ESSENCE OF

TUCSON

-the story-

Written by

Aneta Hebrova

ESSENCE OF TUCSON

-the story-

Written by Aneta Hebrova

Edited by Martha Ames Burgess

Illustrations by Daniel Clint

Cover painting by Andrea Rodriguez

www.essenceoftucson.com

Printed in the U.S.A.

BookBaby • 7905 N. Crescent Blvd • Pennsauken, NJ 08110

First edition, February 2024

To order books: info@essenceoftucson.com

Print ISBN: 979-8-35094-658-1

eBook ISBN: 979-8-35094-651-2

Contents

Please note that this is a simplified, condensed version of a true story.

Journey to the Unknown

I discovered the magic of Tucson by chance during a business trip. As I drove from Saguaro National Park via Gates Pass toward downtown in the late afternoon, the desert landscape's golden glow left me in awe. Witnessing thousands of saguaros bathed in orange light was a truly mystical experience. Compelled by the otherworldly sight that unfolded before me, I had to pull over.

A strange feeling washed over me. For the first time in my life, I felt like I was home. Little did I know at that moment, my life was about to dramatically change, fall apart, and turn upside down.

Approaching my lodgings, I made a stop at the Saguaro Corners restaurant. I chose a seat on the patio and ordered tacos. While enjoying my meal and observing other patrons, my eyes met those of an older, charming woman at a nearby table. A genial smile danced on her lips as she extended a friendly wave, initiating our interaction with a simple "Hi!". I reciprocated with an amiable "Hi," and thus, we began a conversation.

The time melted away as our conversation flowed freely, transcending the bounds of typical small talk. Before I realized it, her husband joined us, seamlessly becoming a part of the dialogue. Together, we savored our meal under the starry desert sky. As the evening advanced, my newfound friends expressed a desire to prolong our discussion.

Curiosity sparked their interest in my plans for Tucson, and I willingly shared my itinerary. "I'm departing Tucson in two days, heading south. However, I do have a free morning the day after tomorrow." The desert night offered respite, suggesting the possibility of shared adventures in Tucson's sun-soaked terrain.

In a gesture of true hospitality, they extended an invitation. "You'll love our terrace. Why not join us for brunch?" they suggested, handing me a card with their contact details—a symbol of their generous offer. I gladly accepted.

Two days later, I typed the address into my navigation system, and my car guided me northwest. Winding through the roads, the GPS directed me upward, unveiling a scenic journey toward the picturesque foothills.

Driving through the Skyline Country Club was a wonderful experience. Lush greenery embellished the manicured landscapes, and elegant homes harmoniously blended into the natural surroundings. The serenity of the area, coupled with the captivating views of the Santa Catalina Mountains, painted a mesmerizing picture as I approached their residence.

I stood at their door, with butterflies of anticipation in my belly, ringing the doorbell. "Come on in! The door is open," they called out. So, I walked inside. The moment my eyes met the breathtaking panorama from their terrace, I was enveloped in another enchanting Tucson magic. The expansive view seemed to stretch beyond the horizon.

As we settled into conversation again, it felt like we had been friends for years, reconnecting after a long separation. I learned that Bob is a retired pilot, and they have been happily married for more than forty years. Both shared a deep love for traveling, which became evident as we exchanged more stories and experiences.

"Well, we need to see each other again," Molly said, her eyes sparkling with enthusiasm as she inquired about my future plans and destinations. While I had some research to do on organic farming and a few business meetings scheduled, I had a three-day stop planned in Sedona in three weeks. "Let me check my calendar" and I shared my plans with them.

"What a coincidence," they exclaimed, "we'll be with our friends in Sedona during those exact same three days! Let's see each other then!"

So, we warmly said our goodbyes and set a date for lunch. The prospect of reuniting in Sedona added an extra layer of excitement to our newfound connection. As I left their terrace, the enchantment of Tucson lingered, and the promise of the future adventures surrounded me with anticipation.

With a positive feeling about these new and exciting plans, I left the beautiful foothills and headed south to one of the farms.

Continuing my journey, I immersed myself in learning about organic farming best practices, natural homes, and the intricacies of aquaponic systems. I was traveling all over Arizona, absorbing knowledge and new experiences.

Three weeks later, we reunited in Sedona for lunch. Our chosen spot was Mesa Grill restaurant at the Sedona Airport, and after enjoying a tasty feast, we decided to explore a nearby vortex situated beneath the airport.

Hiking the short trail, we were met with yet another awe-inspiring scene. Perched on the saddle, we soaked in the panoramic view, sharing beautiful moments amidst the Red Rocks.

As our little adventure concluded, they generously extended an invitation for me to stay in their guest house whenever I came back to Tucson, in exchange for help with the mail and their cats during their own journeys. With this positive conclusion to my Arizona adventure, I returned to Prague.

Call to Adventure

I got back to my office job in the heart of Prague, situated in the Florenc district within the modern office building known as Florentinum. As I gazed out the window, the urban landscape surrounded me with historical architecture and the pulsating rhythm of city life. It stood in stark contrast to the sunny desert I had recently left behind.

Once again, I found myself immersed in the dynamic energy of this bustling city with a medieval feel. The cobblestone streets echoed with the footsteps of pedestrians, and the cityscape boasted buildings and spires that told stories of the past.

My life resumed its normal routine, but not for long. My mind frequently wandered to the Red Rocks, the mountains, the valley, Tucson, and all the adventures that had made me feel alive again. The experiences, like a vivid movie, played in my thoughts, reigniting a sense of vitality. The more I reflected, the more intensely I began to miss those adventures.

After a few weeks, I decided to visit a shaman recommended by a friend, keen to unravel the mysteries of what it all meant. Taking a welcome break from the daily grind, I carefully planned a day off from work. I hopped on a train to a small village in the picturesque countryside.

Following an hour and a half of traveling, I arrived at the doorstep of a quaint villa. As I stepped inside, the atmosphere immediately embraced me with warmth and tranquility. The interior was embellished with antique furniture, tasteful art, and a collection of drums, rattles, and candles that added a touch of mystique to the space. Soon, I settled into a comfortable couch, ready to embark on an enriching experience.

The ambience of the room, rich with ritual instruments, hinted at the profound journey of introspection that lay ahead under the guidance of Tereza, a captivating and wise middle-aged woman. The air was imbued with a sense of serenity, and the room seemed to be infused with the energy of countless stories and insights. As I began sharing my own narrative, I could feel the space becoming a sanctuary for self-discovery and healing, setting the stage for a unique and enlightening encounter.

"That is a profoundly spiritual experience. Let me drum and sing for you, call your guides and connect to your field," she said.

Taking her drum, a beautifully crafted instrument adorned with intricate designs, she began to drum slowly.

Bum, Bum, Bum, Bum, Bum, Bum, a repetitive drumming sound led me to relax.

The resonating beats echoed in the room, creating a mesmerizing rhythm that seemed to transcend time. Her singing and sounds were incredibly natural, reminiscent of a bygone era, invoking a sense of ancient wisdom.

The beating of the drum continued—Bum, Bum, Bum, Bum, Bum, Bum. I felt myself entering a slightly hypnotic state. The room transformed, and an incoherent tapestry of colors and images started to unfold before my eyes.

After she finished drumming, with her eyes closed, she began to say, "In the realm of the unseen, you have received a sacred calling. The spirits of this land have chosen you as their conduit. You are called to return to Tucson, to this place of profound connection and ancient wisdom.

"The spirits speak of a world in transition, of old systems crumbling, and of a changing divine essence. They entrust you with a mission of great significance: to bring healing and transformation to this land, preserving its heritage, and observing the change.

"Your words will be a vessel for conserving the timeless wisdom of this sacred land and the shifting essence of the divine. Through your stories, you will honor the wisdom of the past. This place needs more acknowledgment of what has happened, to witness truth in order to heal. Acknowledgment of the past can bring forgiveness and understanding."

The gravity of the mission ahead unfolded like a sacred scroll, and the path was illuminated with purpose. I was taken aback by what she said. Silence enveloped the room, and, feeling nervous, I scratched my face.

"Why have they chosen me?" I asked.

"Because you've gone through similar experiences, faced life tests requiring forgiveness, and your ancestors also endured genocide. Native Americans will trust you because they sense it, even if you're a 'white gringa.' These things are unseen but deeply felt. Also, because you are not from there, you are an outsider. You will become a bridge between these two worlds."

"I don't speak English that well, and it's so far away. When will this happen, and how will it unfold?" I questioned anxiously.

"Don't worry about the '*how*.' Just trust. Everything will fall into place at the right time. But I need to know if you're willing to accept this mission. Do you want to embark on this journey?"

A profound silence followed. I thought to myself that I had no other choice; if I declined, I would regret it for the rest of my life.

"Okay, I accept," I finally said.

"You have spirit guides who will assist you on this journey," she assured me, and with that, I left her place.

As I sat on the train heading home, a peculiar mix of emotions swirled within me. It was an honor and sounded like a great adventure, but I also felt the weight of the responsibility to fulfill what I had promised. I couldn't share it with anybody. The journey ahead assured both mystery and commitment, and as the landscape outside blurred, the weight of the unseen duty settled into the fabric of my being.

Back at the office, I tried to concentrate on my work, but often I found myself lost in reverie. Vivid images of galloping horses backdropped by orange glow occupied my mind. Even as I strolled through the medieval sections of Prague late in the afternoon on my way home from work, with the iconic Prague Castle in the background—a sight that usually brings me tranquility—I couldn't shake off these persistent thoughts. I even had dreams of cacti and wild open desert nature.

However, as weeks turned into months, nothing significant seemed to happen, and I slowly settled back into my regular routine. I began to doubt if it was all true and if it would ever come to pass.

Then, a few months later, another opportunity arose for me to travel to the USA for business to undertake another research project. I already had friends who offered accommodation in their beautiful place, aligning seamlessly with the guidance Tereza had shared. It unfolded just as she had said.

Before embarking on my journey, I visited her once more, seeking additional information on how to complete the task and what was expected of me. A sense of trepidation lingered within me. Once again, I arrived at the beautiful villa with light blue window-frames and settled into a comfortable sofa. She initiated a drumming session, filling the space with rhythmic beats, and began singing.

"Heja, heja, heeeej," sounded like beautiful ancient melodies, as if the sound itself transcended her presence.

Bum, Bum, Bum, Bum, Bum, Bum. I sank into a deeper state of relaxation. Then, she quieted down and began explaining slowly:

"They want you to write a book."

"What should be the content?" I inquired.

"They want you to bring more truth about history into a special place. It's all very colorful."

"And can they provide any details?"

"The keyword is 'cocktail' or 'essence'. I envision it as a vibrant, colorful substance," she explained, her eyes closed.

"Hmm. I've already written one book with a friend, but I'd like to approach this one completely differently, with more of a cultural focus. But how? What should be in it? I don't know anything about the place. My brain started spinning with more questions."

"They won't tell me more. They'll guide you once you're there. You have to stay alert and look for clues." She disconnected from the guides and asked me,

"Have you seen the movie 'The Limits of Control' by Jim Jarmusch?"

"No," I confessed.

"Watch it. You'll be waiting for clues from strangers, like the mysterious man who's the main character."

"I don't know that one," I replied. "I'll check it out."

A few days later, while watching the movie, I was laughing hysterically at the offbeat scenes. I imagined myself in Tucson, consuming small papers, meeting strangers, and exploring buildings and cafes much like the main character. It all seemed surreal, yet I grasped the concept of staying vigilant and use my imagination. I had no idea what life had in store for me.

Two weeks later, with heightened alertness, I left my Prague apartment in Dejvice, suitcase in hand, and headed for the airport with great anticipation.

Threshold Crossing

The journey had been long, leaving me thoroughly exhausted. Nevertheless, the fatigue disappeared as the familiar faces of Bob and Molly welcomed me at the Tucson airport. A wave of joy washed over me, and it felt wonderful to reunite with them.

My exhaustion seemed to melt away as I settled into the back seat of a luxurious sedan, with Bob taking the driver's seat. Our first stop was at Sauce Pizza & Wine for dinner, and then we continued on to my new, stunning home in the foothills. The desert night unveiled its beauty as we journeyed through the winding roads.

The promise of rest and the embrace of the Southwest's enchanting landscapes welcomed me, setting the stage for the adventures that awaited in the days to come.

Upon crossing the threshold, I experienced an extensive tour of their home. I was taken aback by its beauty. Having relocated from Singapore, their home was designed with a captivating blend of Asian art and Southwestern motifs. It felt like strolling through an art gallery, with each piece of well-crafted furniture exuding an air of elegance and sophistication. It was a home where aesthetic beauty was celebrated, and I discovered learning new words as we explored the place, deeply engaged in the harmonious fusion of cultures within those walls.

Molly mentioned a squeegee, demonstrating its use in cleaning the glass shower wall because I wasn't familiar with the word. "We use it after every shower to prevent water droplets on the glass. It's a nifty tool to keep things sparkling," she explained, kindly offering, "I'll give you one for your shower too."

"Aha, I got it," I replied, recognizing the tool and appreciating their dedication to perfection in creating a space that radiated understated elegance.

My casita, accessible through a private door, revealed itself as a small brick house comprising two rooms: a cozy bedroom and a spacious living area completed with a small built-in kitchen. Particularly noteworthy was a stunning 12 x 5 ft picture window that elegantly framed a breathtaking panoramic view of the entire Tucson landscape. In the foreground, a solitary saguaro stood prominently, adding a touch of natural grandeur to the scene.

Once again, I was utterly overwhelmed with awe. The night view of Tucson, with its luminous lights embellishing the cityscape, left me in wonder from this exceptional vantage point.

Fresh flowers graced my table, and I savored their delicate fragrance before making my way to the shower. Eventually, I snuggled into bed with a cover full of roses. The attention to detail and the thoughtful touches were of a transformational character. The interior was simply perfect and articulated my taste; it surpassed my imagination.

The following morning, I awoke with a surreal sense, as though I had stepped into the role of a character in a movie. It was as if this life were not truly my own.

In an attempt to confirm my reality, I pinched my elbow, feeling a sharp pain that assured me I was wide awake. Filled with eager anticipation to immerse myself in this extraordinary reality, I hurried to the window for another glimpse, keen to relish the awe-inspiring vista of Tucson.

"It's incredible and undeniably real!" I marveled to myself before hopping into the shower, changing into fresh attire, and making my way to their spacious kitchen to greet them.

"Good morning; it's another beautiful day in Tucson," Bob greeted me, just as he did every following morning, while Molly brewed a comforting cup of coffee. It was a delightful start of the day.

We had shopping plans in mind and a strategy to find a second-hand car for me. The ensuing days adhered to a similar routine.

I devoted my mornings to work, acclimating to my new home, and perusing car listings.

It was two to three weeks before I finally purchased a car, giving me the freedom to move around. Amid the whirlwind of these new experiences, I almost forgot about my mission. The words of Tereza returned to my thoughts: "You need to observe the environment and look for clues."

We were on the terrace, surrounded by a lush garden and a shimmering swimming pool. Bob and Molly savored their afternoon glasses of wine while observing the enchanting hummingbirds.

Worry tinged my thoughts as I realized I couldn't sit carefree like them but needed to start working. Determined to kickstart my mission, I pondered where to begin in the vast expanse of Tucson. I took a moment on the terrace, overlooking the town's beauty, and reminded myself to follow the signs, just as I had seen in the movie. The path forward awaited subtle cues from the surroundings.

And then, in the distance, I spotted the symbol "A" on a mountain. "Well, perhaps I should begin with the letter 'A'!" I mused. That evening, I consulted a map and discovered a place called the Mission Garden. It seemed like the perfect starting point for my first expedition.

Tucson's Birthplace, Tohono O'odham & Southwestern Cultures

with Kendall Kroesen, Maegan Lopez, and Jesús Manuel García

I parked my car in front of the old adobe wall structure, which exuded a sense of historical charm, and gazed up at "A" Mountain. From the distant view in Catalina Foothills, the mountain seemed small, and the massive "A" symbol was barely discernible. However, as I approached, it grew larger and more significant.

The garden was tranquil, filled with beautiful plants, tempting me to step inside and take a leisurely walk. The sun was shining, and I was simply enjoying my day, curious about what might happen and who I'd run into.

As a few people passed by, the sun's warmth began to take its toll, so I sought refuge under a *ramada*, a shaded, open-sided structure covered with cacti ribs, and drank some water. I settled down next to a middle-aged man, and we initiated a conversation about this place. He introduced himself as Kendall.

—

Kendall Kroesen holds a Ph.D. in Cultural Anthropology from the University of California, San Diego. Following postdoctoral research roles, he dedicated over 10 years to serving as the Restoration and Urban Program Manager at the Tucson Audubon Society. Currently, Kendall serves as the Community Outreach Coordinator at Mission Garden. His hobbies include bird-watching, culture, gardening, and history.

—

"It's such a lovely place, isn't it? But what's the deal with this garden?" I asked, admiring the surroundings. The air was filled with the earthy scent of soil and the subtle fragrance of blooming flowers. The warm sunlight bathed the garden, casting a golden glow on the plants and pathways.

Kendall began to explain, "Well, one of its main goals is to protect the birthplace of Tucson and educate people about the rich agricultural history of the region. It's a history that's incredibly diverse, shaped by various cultures over the years. We're talking about influences from the original Native Americans—the Hohokam[1], O'odham, Yaqui, through Spanish, Mexican, Chinese, and Anglo to Afro-American communities," counted Kendall on his hand.

"It's a real melting pot of agricultural traditions, and the garden's here to showcase and preserve that heritage."

I was impressed with his knowledge; I asked for his permission and tapped the audio record button on my mobile phone. This marked my first interview.

"What a diversity! How old is this place, though?"

Kendall continued, "Well, the inhabitants of this part of the Santa Cruz River flood plain have been practicing agriculture for over 4000 years, making it the longest continuously cultivated site in North America. That's quite something. And you're right, the garden serves as an educational resource by preserving biodiversity and showcasing cultural heritage that might otherwise be forgotten and lost. It's essential, especially with today's focus on high-yield crops in commercial agriculture, which is leading to a loss of variety and tastes.

----

[1] According to current distinctions made by O'odham Elders, Hohokam is the term that archeologists use to describe the culture represented by the artifacts that they have found buried in lands now occupied by the O'odham and other cultures. The term Huhugam is a term used by the O'odham themselves referring to the ancestral people who lived here before.

"If you're up for it, I can take you on a tour," Kendall suggested, and I enthusiastically agreed.

As we strolled through the garden, Kendall continued, "The Early Agriculture Garden features more primitive varieties of squash, corn, beans, and ancestral plants like *chiltepin*, which is an ancestor of chili peppers. In the Hohokam Garden, you'll find more advanced varieties of corn, squash, beans, as well as cotton and agave. The Pre-contact O'odham Garden represents the period before colonization by the Spanish, where you can also find amaranth, tobacco, tepary beans, and more." He was truly excited and kept walking further.

"So, 'pre-contact' means before the missionaries came? You're illustrating here the evolution of crops over time, right?" I asked.

"Exactly," Kendall replied. "The Post-contact O'odham Garden showcases the evolution of O'odham gardening, with the adoption of new European crops. When Spanish colonists and missionaries arrived in the 1690s, they brought a variety of Old World crops such as pomegranate, fig, quince, Seville orange, grape, and different types of legumes. The Mexican Garden features more tropical plants like papaya, various herbs, and fruits from farther south.

"Chinese farmers introduced bottle gourd, bitter melon, and luffa. We also have two special gardens: the Moore Medicinal Garden, dedicated to local medicinal plants, and the Tomorrow's Garden, focusing on forward-looking growing techniques like hydroponics and vertical farming. Our most recent project is a newly built canal, which reintroduces some of the floodplain features to the garden and serves as a refuge for endangered fish species, including the Gila topminnow."

"Wow, that's very interesting. But why is the birthplace of Tucson in this area?" I wondered.

Kendall explained, casting a glance at the "A" Mountain, "The reason this is Tucson's birthplace is both the period of four thousand years of continuous agriculture and the existence of a large

Native American village here when the Spanish colonists arrived. The colonists and missionaries decided this would be another missionary outpost. The name of the Native American village here was 'S-cuk-Şon,' which means 'spring at the base of the black mountain,' referring to the dark volcanic rock on a nearby mountain. And that's where the name Tucson originated."

"That's fascinating," I remarked. "What's the evidence supporting that 4000-year history?"

Kendall replied, "In the archaeological record, over 4000 years ago, they started seeing denser populations along the Santa Cruz River and the remains of temporary houses that were occupied during the growing season. In one of these houses, they found maize remains, one of which was radiocarbon dated to 4100 years ago. When archaeologists dug trenches, they found the shapes of canal remains dating back at least 3500 years ago. They knew people were channeling water from the wetlands, as there was a wetland just close by here to the south. They were building the canals to channel water to their cornfields, so there is a lot of evidence."

"I had no idea that this place had such a rich history. How did you manage to find the original seeds and plants?" I asked, curious about the preservation efforts as we walked through a quince orchard.

"We conducted extensive research on what was cultivated during different historical periods and within various cultural traditions. Some of the original trees brought by the Spanish colonists still thrive in Southern Arizona. While the original trees may not have endured, many of their descendants remain. These trees may be genetically identical, as they have been propagated from cuttings, making them genetic clones of their parent trees.

"We believe we have preserved nearly exact varieties of these trees, and perhaps even the same genetic individuals, through a program known as the Kino Heritage Fruit Trees Project. Additionally, we're fortunate in Tucson to have a non-profit seed bank called Native Seeds/SEARCH. This organization has been collecting heritage crops from across the Southwestern United States and Northern Mexico for decades. All of these factors contributed to Tucson's recognition as a City of Gastronomy by UNESCO, a title held by only two cities in the USA."

Our conversation flowed seamlessly as we continued discussing agriculture, Indigenous cultures, and the significance of preserving these traditions. I also shared with Kendall the experiences and insights I had gathered during my research trip across Arizona.

"You know, I would love to speak with some members of the Tohono O'odham Nation. Do you happen to know anyone from that tribe?"

Kendall nodded: "Yes, I do. You should talk to Maegan, she works here. She's from the tribe and can provide you with her perspective."

Keen to connect with Maegan, I waited with anticipation as Kendall called out to someone nearby, asking, "Where is Maegan? Is she here today?"

The response came swiftly, "Yes, she's over there!" With that, Kendall shook my hand and headed toward Meagan to let her know to come to me, as he needed to attend to his duties.

In the quiet moments before Maegan's arrival, I absorbed the details of the garden. The soil beneath my feet seemed to cradle centuries of stories, and the plants whispered tales of resilience and adaptation. The sunlight played hide-and-seek through the leaves, casting dancing shadows on the pathways.

—

Maegan Lopez comes from New Fields in the Tohono O'odham Nation. She earned her Bachelor of Science degree in Family Studies and Human Development from the University of Arizona and boasts extensive experience working with the Tribal Health Department. Maegan serves a crucial role at Mission Garden as a Gardener and Cultural Outreach Liaison, leveraging her knowledge to contribute to the preservation and revitalization of traditional agricultural practices.

—

A young and amiable woman, wearing a hat and sunglasses, approached me, and together we decided to take a stroll through the garden. Despite the late afternoon hour and the intense heat, we opted to sit beneath another ramada in the garden to extend our conversation.

As we settled into the shade, I introduced myself and briefly shared my background, expressing my strong interest in acquiring more knowledge because I'm working on a book. I also recounted my initial experiences when I arrived here, how it made me feel like I had found my true home.

The ramada offered a comfortable refuge from the sun, and as we sat there surrounded by the vibrant colors of the garden, the atmosphere encouraged a deeper exchange of stories and insights. The rustling of leaves and the occasional chirping of birds created a natural symphony in the background.

"I've always had this yearning to explore beyond my village. I never really wanted to live in the village where I came from. I've always aspired to follow in my grandpa's footsteps. He was a gardener and lived in a different part of the Tohono O'odham reservation," Maegan shared.

"So, what does 'Tohono O'odham' actually mean?" I asked curiously.

And Maegan began to explain: "It means People of the Desert. Once I started to learn more about Nature—the plants, desert, animals—and tried to find my own way, figuring out 'where do I fit in all of this'… It is in our name, we are the People of the Desert!

"We have to remember that we cannot be one without the other. I feel like, as Desert People, the desert will not survive without us. If we are all suddenly gone as Desert People, I don't think it will be much time before these plants are gone too and vice versa. If we forget who we are, if we just adapt to the Western lifestyle and absolutely let it all go, I don't think this desert will survive very much longer. So, it's really important to ignite that within us and remind ourselves we don't live within a reservation—that Nature is all around us and it has no borders."

"That's a beautiful perspective. You originally didn't have any borders. So, what happened when the missionaries came? How did they persuade your people to adapt, and how do you perceive that?"

"When I was in school, I had the exact same question. How did this happen to such a massive crowd of people? During the post-contact period, our population was significantly larger. We inhabited a vast landmass comparable in size to Connecticut.

"I just couldn't wrap my head around this. How would they persuade them? My instructor at that time explained to me that the truth is that in most cases, our population growth occurred under duress. The Spanish arrived on horseback, as foreigners, equipped with shiny metal armor and swords. They gathered all the revered people, the medicine people, and they cut off their heads in front of the entire community, in front of all the O'odham people. They declared, 'You have no power now. We are taking it.'

"This was their prevailing strategy. If you kill the most valuable people, the rest will bend to the Spanish and this explanation makes sense to me.

"So, contrary to what is taught in our schools, history reveals a different story about how we yielded to the Spanish. In the book 'At the Border of Empires' by A. Marak and L. Tuennerman, which chronicles the period when various governments were influencing the Tohono O'odham people and attempting to assimilate them into Western culture, three types of governments emerged: the Spanish, the Mexican, and the American. Each approached us from different angles, and those closest to these influences adopted the respective narratives and ways of life.

"Consequently, we now have sub-groups within our tribal communities that uphold different beliefs. Protestants, Catholics, Lutherans—different kinds of religious ideologies are embedded in

21

the government's ideology. This massive cultural change not only influenced the people and their culture but also the land."

I asked, "How did your community maintain its traditions during this difficult period?"

"We relied on medicine people and Elders within our community to preserve our traditions," she replied. "However, until 1979, there was a ban on religious freedom, so traditional ceremonies had to be performed in secret. Reviving these practices took time and effort."

I was curious how Native Americans got here, and about her perspective on that, so I asked: "How do you believe your people were created?"

"So, with the origin stories and how we grew up as O'odham people, our understanding is that we tell the stories only during winter. We were taught that animals and all beings that live with us in this desert protect something—they all have a purpose. We all grew up knowing certain things have purposes.

"Animals, particularly those that sleep during the night but become active in the heat and hibernate in winter, like gila monsters, tarantulas, and snakes, play a role in protecting our stories because they are considered sacred. Therefore, we refrain from telling stories during this time, especially in the summer when they are active.

"We only tell stories during the winter when they're sleeping, so we don't get attacked. It's a tradition rooted in wisdom, a precautionary measure to avoid drawing unwanted attention. Among the narratives that resonates through the stillness, the most sacred is the tale of our origin, a tale of the Earth Maker, the Elder Brother— known to us as I'itoi."

Maegan stopped. "Oh, somebody's dog" she said. We both looked at the dog that was barking and approached us to be comforted. "See, I hope he is not an omen," Maegan laughed and added: "He is like, 'No girl, don't tell her!'"

The dog left and Maegan continued, "Well, I'itoi created everybody, giving us this philosophy called Himdag, which means 'The Way of Life.' The philosophy is to teach us how to live in this harsh environment, survive with the plants and animals, and keep moving forward throughout the generations. As long as the Earth exists, you will know how to survive it.

"I'itoi, the Earth Maker, guided our ancestors in living in this harsh environment, teaching them how to navigate life's challenges. There's a special story about our people turning into saguaros, but I can't share all the details now. The saguaros have a purpose here in the Sonoran Desert, and it's because of that story that we honor them. They symbolize resilience and continuity in our shared history."

"It's fascinating how your culture reveres the saguaro cactus."

"Yes, the saguaro cactus is the heart of our culture. We hold a ceremony every season when its fruit blossoms. We pick and prepare the fruit, sing songs, and dance—bringing the community together. We respect everything that comes from the saguaro. We also believe this ceremony brings rain, an essential aspect of maintaining balance in nature. We also follow the Tohono O'odham Calendar for planting and celebrating new community members, creating a strong bond with the land and each other."

There was a small symbol on her T-shirt. "What does this symbol mean?" I asked.

"Oh that's 'Man in the Maze'. This symbol brings in all those main core concepts, which is surviving and knowing that you have a purpose in all of this. Knowing that our life is going to be like that—similar to a labyrinth—with all these twists and turns, we never know what is going to come around the bend, but we keep going until we get to the center. That center represents the end of life and the beginning of a brand new one. So, that's how that symbol, as far as I understand, brings all these different things together. Personally, seeing the symbol brings me back to these essential truths we tend to forget in our daily lives, emphasizing our shared goal to live a meaningful life."

As someone approached us with questions about the garden, Maegan excused herself, assuring me that she would be back soon. Left alone with my own thoughts, I took a moment to absorb the surroundings. The late afternoon sun cast a warm glow on the vibrant blooms and vegetation of the Mission Garden. The soft murmur of a nearby water feature added a soothing ambiance, and the occasional rustle of leaves hinted at a gentle breeze. Seated under the ramada, I marveled at the resilience of the desert flora and the sense of history preserved in this carefully tended space.

When Maegan returned, we exchanged goodbyes because she had to get back to work, and I left, my heart filled with inspiration and hope. This day not only deepened my understanding of the Mission Garden but also reassured me that, hopefully, I could fulfill the promises made on this journey.

—

Bob and Molly were exceptional hosts, making me feel truly welcomed. Molly would pick fresh roses from the garden every week and arrange them on the dining table. Our mornings sometimes commenced by savoring the delightful scents and diverse varieties of these beautiful blooms, ranging from white and light pink to dark shades.

Bob went the extra mile to make me feel at home. He installed a temperature gauge on my terrace, displaying both Fahrenheit and

Celsius, so that I could learn the nuances. Their attention to detail and perfectionist approach made my stay truly memorable.

During that time, my daily routine followed a predictable pattern. Mornings were dedicated to work, and after lunch, in the serene moments when everyone in Prague was winding down, I found solace from phone calls and the freedom to explore.

These explorations were often spontaneous, with no pre-determined plan. Inspired by Jim Jarmusch's movie, I would hop into my car and let intuition be my guide, relishing the luxury of having no agenda. This led me to discover fascinating gardens, cozy cafes, and art galleries. Chance encounters with locals who shared intriguing insights about Tucson added unexpected dimensions to my explorations. In this blend of work and adventure, the days passed swiftly.

One evening, I decided to break from my usual routine and tuned into a local PBS channel. A captivating man named Jesús Manuel García appeared on the screen, speaking passionately about the Sonoran Desert. Fascinated, I felt a strong desire to engage in a conversation with him. When I reached out and asked if we could meet, to my surprise, he proposed the Mission Garden, with which he had an association. So, once again, I was driving to the Mission Garden.

—

Jesús Manuel García holds a Bachelor's degree in Ecology and Evolutionary Biology, with a minor in Cultural Anthropology. Since 1991, he has been working for Arizona-Sonora Desert Museum, serving as a Conservation Research Associate. He is also the Director of the Kino Heritage Fruit Trees program. Jesús' many interests include conservation biology, music, drawing, cultural ecology, languages, and gardening.

—

Jesús and I set up a meeting in the educational building in the back of Mission Garden, seeking shelter from the heat outside. Meeting him in person, he appeared remarkably similar to how I had seen him on television—incredibly vital and knowledgeable. He gave off the impression that he didn't adhere to the usual schedule of ordinary people due to the abundance of his interests.

We started our conversation with a discussion about music, specifically polka, which is traditional Tohono O'odham music that accompanies the "chicken scratch." Interestingly, it actually has Czech origins, adopted by Native Americans when Eastern European immigrants brought their accordions with them to work on the railroads.

The blend of cultures and the evolution of traditions fascinated me, and Jesús shared insights into the intricate connections that have shaped the cultural landscape of the area.

"You don't speak Spanish, right?" Jesús asked me while showing some videos with Mexican music.

"No." I replied and laughed in my mind because I also seen a violin like it was shown in "The Limits of Control" movie. I knew I was on the right path.

"You know, you can trace a lot of history through music; it tells you about immigration. The original Native American music is quite simple: just drums and flutes. But European influences brought in guitars, violins, accordions, fiddles, and harps—all string instruments. It expanded the musical repertoire and allowed for greater complexity in the music, it created new melodies and arrangements. This cultural exchange enriched the musical landscape."

"It's really fascinating. I would have never expected our traditional folk music to find a connection here. It is such a blend!"

Given Jesús' reputation as a Sonoran Desert expert, I couldn't resist asking more questions about this unique environment.

"So, why is the Sonoran Desert called Sonoran?"

"Well, there are several reasons behind that," Jesús explained.

"Around 150 years ago, this area used to be a part of Sonora, which was part of Mexico. Most of the territory that we know now as Arizona, California, parts of Nevada and Colorado, New Mexico, and Utah was actually Mexican territory. In 1849, a war broke out between Mexico and the United States, leading to the United States winning and these parts becoming part of the United States. However, the story of border changes is more complex than that.

"This region was acquired as part of the Gadsden Purchase from Mexico, with the original border in Phoenix. Due to the absence of a river serving as a natural landmark, a line was drawn across the desert, establishing the current border. Before the mid-1800s, this entire area was referred to as the Properties of Sonora. Southern Arizona and California were just small portions of the larger Sonoran Desert, which is primarily in Mexico."

Curious about what made this region so unique, I asked Jesús, and he became unstoppable in his explanation.

"Going beyond cultural aspects, the Sonoran Desert is part of four deserts identified in North America, along with the Mohave Desert, Great Basin Desert, and Chihuahuan Desert. So, you have four deserts, and out of all these four deserts, the Sonoran Desert is the most biodiverse desert in North America, if not in the whole world. It boasts unique features like two rainy seasons, extreme summer and winter, and a unique latitude location—exactly at the 32 degrees latitude, where north prevailing winds flow in a way that brings quite a bit of water here. Not a lot compared to other places, but it is an average of 12 inches (25 centimeters) a year, which is still pretty significant. So, it's very hot, very cold, very dry, and very wet. All these elements working together make this place unique, bringing biodiversity of plants, animals, and cultural diversity of people."

"It's a remarkable place. But what about the cultural aspects of the Southwest? Can you tell me more about the Southwestern cultures?"

"I often joke around because people call this area Southwest. If you ask any American, they say, 'I live in the Southwest,' and that includes California, Arizona, and New Mexico, but for us

Mexicans—I mean, it depends who you are talking to—for us, this is not Southwest, it's Northwest.

"So, I am trying to describe the perspectives of the people.

"Now this is when you talk to Mexicans, but what happens when you talk to Native Americans? Do they call it Southwest? No.

"Do they call it Northwest? No.

"They simply call it the center of the universe, they call it *home*.

"I always try to put into perspective the cultural values of the region before naming a place or talking about location, and we really have to start acknowledging that we are on the ancestral lands of Indigenous people, the Tohono O'odham in this case.

"To simplify things, we can say Native Americans were here first, European Hispanics came in next, and then Anglo-Saxon culture entered. But if we talk about Native Americans, it's not just one group. There are dozens of cultural and linguistic groups, who lived here in the region.

"If we discuss Hispanics coming in here, there were not only Spanish, but Germans, African slaves, a Jewish influence from Central Eastern Europe, and then you have the Anglo-Saxon culture coming in from the eastern United States. However, it wasn't just them either. They were probably mixed with Mormons, English, other Europeans, a few Africans, and Chinese, and that's just the beginning within historical terms in the last 100 years. Now in the last 2-3 decades, we have refugees from Iraq, Somalia, Afghanistan, Kenya, and that blend continues to increase as we speak. So, it is international."

Jesús was in his element, excitedly sharing his extensive knowledge about the desert's history and culture. I was captivated by our conversation, savoring every nugget of information.

Time flew by, and I ended up spending another hour with Jesús, engrossed in an exchange of endless ideas and insights. Eventually, we said our goodbyes, and I departed feeling enriched by the encounter.

As I drove happily back to the foothills, I couldn't help but reflect on the invaluable lessons I had learned during our conversation. The desert was no longer just a landscape; it had evolved into a vibrant tapestry of stories and traditions, and I felt privileged to have glimpsed a small piece of it.

Road of Trials

Molly and I developed a strong bond during my stay. On afternoons at our free disposal, we ventured on extensive hikes, exploring numerous trails that stretched from east to west. From the captivating beauty of Sabino Canyon and Ventana Canyon, to the challenging Finger Rock Trail, and the serene paths of Pima Canyon, we left no route unexplored. We even did a little adventure to Catalina State Park, wandering through the fields of wild poppies. It wasn't just about the trails; there was a sense that our lives had crossed paths before, like some cosmic connection.

One vivid memory stands out - an encounter in Pima Canyon. Molly suddenly stopped in her tracks, her eyes gleaming with a distant recollection. She described having a vivid mental flash of us walking together, lightly dressed, and foraging for herbs. What struck her as uncanny was her observation of a belt filled with small pouches around her waist, used to collect these herbs. Each pouch seemed designed for gathering herbs for a tribe we seemed to be aiding in some bygone era. It was a mystical connection that bound us, bridging the gap between our present lives and those we had led in a time long past.

Bob and Molly both played crucial roles in ensuring I felt comfortable and had everything I needed during my stay. They wanted me to fully embrace the American way of life, and I appreciated their efforts. However, there were moments when it became a bit overwhelming. In our cooking sessions, Molly would cheerfully say, "It's not tomatoes, it's tomaaatoeesss! Open your mouth properly!" I was grateful for their guidance, but my brain could only handle so much English.

After two months, I started to feel pressured. Especially during evenings, my brain rebelled, going on strike and rendering me incapable of responding. There were moments when my mind froze, like a computer processor under too much stress. Even watching a movie seemed like a daunting task, leading me to seek solace in my casita. I started listening to audios, but I struggled with understanding some words. Frustration and desperation kicked in, making me abandon books and dictionaries—I just wanted to escape it all!

During these vulnerable moments, I found solace in a secret retreat on the patio or venturing onto the golf course, where a unique nocturnal world unfolded.

From my east-facing terrace, the moon emerged majestically from the Santa Catalina Mountains, casting a luminous glow over the landscape. Its reflection shimmered in the stillness of the pool. I was captivated by its slow, rhythmic journey across the heavens, a silent witness to its celestial dance.

Under the moonlit sky, javelinas congregated by the fountain, sipping water, while owls maintained a silent vigil from the trees, and bats danced through the night air. The distant howls of coyotes added a haunting melody to the nocturnal symphony, creating an atmosphere both eerie and enchanting. It was such a relief not to think, translate or memorize and just observe.

On nights without a full moon, I casually strolled to the clubhouse. Occasionally, I dared to explore the pool area, where I lounged, transfixed by the stars and the ethereal beauty of the Milky Way. As I gazed at the monochromatic display above, I marveled at the night sky, wondering how astrophotographers could capture the vibrant hues that eluded my naked eye, painting the cosmos in unseen colors. Intrigued by this cosmic mystery, I embarked on a quest that led me to the captivating world of Adam Block, whom I decided to contact the next day.

Night Skies, Feathered Friends & Giant Cacti

with Adam Block, Luke Safford, and William Peachey

———

Adam Block is an astronomer and award-winning astrophotographer. He graduated from the University of Arizona in Astronomy and Physics in 1996. Following his graduation, he was employed by the Kitt Peak National Observatory to develop the newly created public observatory programs and later founded the Mount Lemmon SkyCenter for the University of Arizona. In 2012, he received the Hubble Award, a prestigious honor for excellence in astro-photography.

———

Adam and I decided to meet at Exo Roast Coffee on 6th Avenue. When he laid out some of his work, it became clear that our small table wouldn't do justice to the galactic wonders he captured. We laughed about the space constraints and agreed that the universe deserves a bit more room.

As we settled in, I started sharing about my background and the twists of fate that brought me to Tucson. Naturally, my curiosity turned to Adam's journey.

"So, astronomy has been your passion from a young age?"

Adam smiled, "Absolutely. The sky and astronomy, that was my thing even as a young child. It all started when I got my first kids' compact telescope when I was six for Christmas. That day, I knew I would become an astronomer."

I was captivated, "And when did photography come into the picture?"

He leaned back, recalling his journey, "Well, like most young astronomers, my early interest was in getting a small telescope, looking through it at the sky. But then I discovered in books and magazines that there were ways to capture what I was seeing. For me, that became a compelling idea because it was a way to share it with others. I always wanted to show people what I found cool. So, around the age of twelve, I got a camera that attached to the telescope, and that's when it all started."

"That's exciting! Why is Tucson so good for stargazing?"

"This region, especially the southwest, with a spotlight on Arizona, and you can extend it to include California and New Mexico, offers an ideal climate. It regularly boasts clear skies, a boon for astronomy. But it's not just that; there are mountains here where observatories can be strategically placed. This is crucial because you're dealing with less severe atmospheric conditions that result in less light distortion.

"Additionally, this part of the world has the necessary infrastructure—universities and institutions that actively support scientific endeavors. Building a telescope in remote places can be challenging due to the maintenance requirements."

I nodded, absorbing the information. "So, what's the stargazing experience like at the Mt. Lemmon SkyCenter and Kitt Peak National Observatory?"

Adam's eyes lit up, "It's more than just peering through a telescope; it's an immersive experience that spans a few hours. Both programs start with an introduction, providing you with an awe-inspiring overview of your place in the universe. You then get to enjoy a light dinner and witness a spectacular sunset from the mountain's summit.

"After dark, the real cosmic journey begins. People learn about the myriad of wonders in the heavens above, starting with binocular observations that you get to use throughout the evening.

"Later, you'll peer through the telescope to see various natural phenomena—planets, stars, constellations, galaxies, and nebulae. At Kitt Peak, you gaze through a 20-inch telescope, and at Mt. Lemmon SkyCenter, it's a 32-inch telescope—one of the largest accessible to the public.

"There are very few places in the world where you can observe stars under the same quality conditions that professionals enjoy."

"Can you see further away with a 32-inch telescope?"

Adam clarified, "Not entirely, it's not about distance. A bigger telescope collects more light. The more light you collect, the easier it is to see through the telescope or capture a better image. So, more light means more information. A nebula would appear brighter. From the Mt. Lemmon Sky Center, we can show nebulae or galaxies that you wouldn't be able to see through a smaller telescope.

"At Mt. Lemmon SkyCenter, I can show unique celestial sights like NGC 4490, a pair of interacting galaxies. Other public programs often lack the right conditions or a big enough telescope for such views. Mt. Lemmon SkyCenter provides a one-of-a-kind experience."

"In the sky, what can you see, and which objects are the farthest away?"

Adam shared enthusiastically, "There's an entire universe to see. Besides the planets and stars, we show various objects like star clusters, galaxies, nebulae, and more. There are astronomical events like storms on Jupiter, meteor showers, lunar eclipses, bright comets in the sky, and much more. And when it comes to distance, there are objects like quasars, typically galaxies with black holes in their centers that emit lots of radiation. These galaxies can be seen across vast distances, billions of light years away."

Curious, I asked, "How is it possible that pictures from the universe can't be detected in color with our eyes?"

Adam explained patiently, "The problem is always an eyeball, because they are not designed to do this stuff. Our eyes are not very good detectors of light at low light levels. When you are in your room at night to go to sleep and you turn off the lights, all of the color seems to disappear. However, nothing changes if you take a long exposure with a digital camera in your room. The resulting picture will have all of the colors as normal!

"So when the light level is below a certain threshold the cone cells of our eyes (the color receptors) do not perceive the different colors of light. This is why most things look gray through a telescope. There are very few astronomical objects that are bright enough to see striking color. There are exceptions though.

"Planets reflect sunlight, showcasing their colors. Stars and some nebulae are bright enough for us to observe their colors through a telescope. However, many distant and faint objects can't be seen easily. Sensitive CCD cameras capture this light, creating stunning pictures of the Universe. Some may think these images are not real colors, but it's more accurate to say that when you look through a telescope, those wavelengths of light are reaching your eyes, even if you can't see them. It's not that cameras enhance the light; our eyes have limitations in perceiving certain wavelengths."

I pondered, "When is the best time to go stargazing?"

Adam advised, "The best time in this region is late summer, fall, and winter. These months offer clearer skies and reduced light pollution. Make sure to choose nights coinciding with a new moon or when the moon is not visible—a moonless night—to enhance the experience. This ensures that the moon's radiant glow doesn't overshadow the brilliance of stars and other heavenly objects, allowing observers to fully immerse themselves in the cosmic spectacle."

My meeting with Adam came to an end, while my fascination with the stars continued to grow. The charm of the experience lingered, so I signed up for the five-hour public program.

And a few days later, driven by curiosity, I set out on the road to Mt. Lemmon SkyCenter. The late afternoon drive up to Mt.

Lemmon turned into a delightful adventure, showcasing the mesmerizing transformation of saguaros into pine trees right before my eyes—an enchanting metamorphosis that unfolded in less than 40 minutes.

About twelve of us gathered, forming an intimate group for the stargazing program. The evening began with an interesting astronomy lecture, delving into the wonders of the cosmos and adding layers to my understanding of the night sky. The atmosphere was charged with curiosity and anticipation as we absorbed every detail shared by the knowledgeable guide.

After a small dinner, our group had the chance to get to know each other and chat. Following the meal, we stepped outside to witness the breathtaking sunset. As the sun dipped below the horizon, its warm glow painted the landscape, setting the stage for the celestial spectacle to come.

Our guide skillfully wielded a laser pointer, tracing the intricate patterns of constellations overhead. It felt like connecting the dots in the vast canvas of the night sky. Equipped with binoculars, we continued our journey, exploring the celestial marvels that graced the cosmic expanse above us.

The pinnacle of the night arrived as we took turns peering through the Schulman 32-inch telescope. This powerful instrument opened portals to distant worlds, unveiling the mysteries of neighboring planets, galaxies, and nebulae, millions of light-years away. The guide's expertise added depth to the experience, providing insights that enhanced our appreciation for the cosmic wonders.

The evening had a profound impact on me. Now, when I step outside in the dark, there's a sense that something truly celestial is above me. The stars, once distant, now feel like old friends, and the vastness of the universe is comforting in its grandeur.

—

Not long after this experience, I shared it with Bob and Molly, and Bob kindly lent me his binoculars to continue observing the night sky.

A few days later, fueled by spontaneous curiosity, I grabbed the binoculars during daylight hours and stumbled upon a new, yet-to-be-discovered passion—birds! As I scanned the surroundings, I was captivated by the vibrant avian life that had previously gone almost unnoticed.

There were bird feeders on the patio, attracting regular visits from hummingbirds and quails. However, as I walked towards the other side of the terrace, under a little bush, I discovered a completely new species of birds that I had never seen before!

From the subtle Cactus Wren to colorful species such as the fiery orange male Vermillion Flycatcher and the punk-esque appearance of a male Pyrrhuloxia, and the distinctive sound of a Northern Mockingbird, I was utterly blown away.

Excited about my newfound passion for birdwatching, I explored the Tucson Audubon Society online and discovered Sweetwater Wetlands as a potential destination. Intrigued by their upcoming field trips, I decided to join one, and that's where I met Luke Safford.

———

Luke Safford's birding passion began at age six in Washington State, nurtured by his grandparents. Establishing a life list early on, he moved to Arizona in 2015, making Sweetwater Wetlands his go-to birding spot. As the Director of

Engagement and Education at the Tucson Audubon Society, Luke leads weekly walks, coordinates events, and shares his love for birds with the community.

———

Joining a group of birders at the Sweetwater Wetlands field trip was a great experience. The enthusiasts were equipped with hats, binoculars slung across their chests, and notepads peeking out of their pockets. Our guide, Luke, led the way, and we followed him. As we strolled along, I couldn't help but think that spotting these birders in their distinctive gear wasn't as challenging as finding some of the elusive birds they were so expertly tracking.

Sweetwater Wetlands, covering about 60 acres, serves as both a sewage treatment facility with the best euphemistic name 'Sweetwater' and a thriving wildlife sanctuary. This unique dual-purpose site utilizes ponds, marshes, and riparian habitats to create a diverse ecosystem, attracting various bird species. Towering mesquite trees add a touch of grandeur, and the graceful sway of cattails completes the picturesque landscape, providing a haven for both water treatment and natural beauty.

After a short walk and pointing out a few species, we found a shaded spot to rest and we bombarded Luke with questions, excited to absorb his wealth of knowledge about birding.

"So, Luke, when's the best time for birding in Tucson?"

Luke adjusted his cap and began: "Birding is fantastic year-round in Tucson, but my favorite months for birding are August and April. August falls in the middle of our monsoon season, and yes, it is hot, but the rain provides food resources in the form of insects and flowering plants for the many bird species still in nesting mode, migrating birds already headed south, and post-breeding dispersal species. August tends to be the easiest time to find specialty birds like the Five-striped Sparrow, and hummingbird diversity reaches its peak, with up to 10-11 species seen regularly, possibly more. April falls in the middle of spring migration, and our canyons come alive with migrating warblers and returning Elegant Trogons. Elf Owls and other night birds are most vocal during this month as well."

"What about migration cycles? When does it all happen?" asked an older man from a crowd.

"Spring migration starts in early March with returning Bell's Vireos and Lucy's Warblers and continues throughout the month, with good numbers of hawks coming north along the Santa Cruz River. This is the best area in the world for seeing large numbers of migrating Common Black Hawks. April and May are busy for migrants with the last breeding birds, Yellow-billed Cuckoo and Sulphur-bellied Flycatcher, arriving in late May and early June. Fall migration starts early with hummingbirds arriving from their breeding grounds as early as late July. Flycatchers and warblers pass through in August and September, with most of our breeding birds leaving by middle of September. In November we'll start seeing flocks of Sandhill Cranes arriving in the Sulphur Springs Valley, along with other wintering birds like longspurs and waterfowl."

Then someone asked "Alright, so what about rare birds? What should I keep an eye out for?"

Luke's eyes lit up. "The habitats of Southeast Arizona attract many species of birds not seen anywhere else in the United States, and while they may be rare in the U.S. they often are common in many areas in Mexico. The number one bird that attracts birders to Tucson and Southeast Arizona is the Elegant Trogon. Its colorful plumage (red, green, and coppery-colored tail) and croaking call give it a very tropical appearance that is unlike anything else you'll see in the United States.

"Other specialty birds include Montezuma Quail, Rivoli's Hummingbird, Violet-crowned Hummingbird, Rose-throated Becard, Red-faced Warbler, and Rufous-capped Warbler. Rarer birds like Berylline Hummingbird, White-throated Thrush, and Flame-colored Tanager attract thousands of birders within days of being found."

"And where are the go-to spots in Tucson for birding?" was my question.

"Of course, this place, Sweetwater Wetlands is my top pick. A two hour tour will often result in 30 - 50 species of birds depending on the season with Southeast Arizona specialties like Gambel's Quail, Gila Woodpecker, Verdin, and Abert's Towhee being common year-round. In breeding season a birder will find Tropical Kingbirds and Lucy's Warblers nesting in the willows and mesquites.

"Or within about an hour of Tucson you can visit Madera Canyon in the Santa Rita Mountains where Elegant Trogons nest in warm season, Painted Redstarts flit about in the oaks, and Sulphur-bellied Flycatchers 'squeak' away from the tops of sycamores. The Santa Rita Lodge is a great place to stay and has numerous hummingbird and seed feeders out for birds and all people to enjoy.

"Also, the 25-mile drive up the Catalina Highway starts in northeast Tucson begins in the Sonoran Desert and climbs up, traversing six life zones, where you finish near the top of Mt. Lemmon in mixed conifer forest. It is equivalent biologically to traveling from Mexico to Canada! One can see upwards of 100 species on a spring day on this route, from Zone-tailed Hawk to Steller's Jay to Scott's Oriole."

Feeling inspired, I also asked for some practical tips. "Any advice for a newbie birder like me?"

Luke replied: "Check out the Southern Arizona Birding Festival organized by Tucson Audubon Society—it's a birder's haven. And grab 'Finding Birds in Southeast Arizona' also by Tucson Audubon. It's a goldmine with maps, site descriptions, and bird expectations. Consider hiring a local guide for an extra level of expertise; it can make all the difference in spotting those life-list birds."

Our 2 hour-long walk through Sweetwater Wetlands revealed a multitude of bird species, leaving me thoroughly thrilled, because we counted 32 species of birds.

With a head buzzing full of newfound knowledge, I thanked Luke and the group members for the crash course in Tucson birding. As I left the Sweetwater Wetlands, I couldn't wait to dive deeper into the vibrant world of birds.

—

Weeks slipped by as I focused on work, and Bob and Molly's frequent travels kept them away. In their absence, I took care of the cats. The solitude, initially calm, eventually began to feel a bit too lonely.

To break free from the quietude, I attended a few networking events. One evening, seeking a change of scenery, I was drawn to the lively Borderlands Brewery for the Green Drinks gathering of nature advocates.

The atmosphere buzzed with conversations among nature enthusiasts, creating an inviting backdrop. As I settled onto the outdoor patio, the gathering gained momentum, with more people arriving to share their passion for the environment. Amidst the crowd, an older man took a seat next to me.

He introduced himself as Bill, and our conversation quickly shifted to the topic of saguaro cacti. With his animated storytelling, he spoke clearly, punctuating his narratives, making it easy for me to grasp the nuances of the discussion. Captivated by his lively demeanor, I decided to stick around, eager to absorb more of Bill's fascinating stories and insights.

—

William Peachey, also known as Bill, studied geology at the University of Arizona and has been an independent scientist and speleologist for most of his life, focusing on saguaros and the caves of Arizona. His recent Saguaro bloom study spans over 20 years of research, and he has also delved into the anatomy and pests of the saguaro. Serving as an advisor to the Biosphere 2, Arizona-Sonora Desert Museum, and organizations like the Disney Corporation and the video series Nature, he is an expert on the local environment and ecology.

—

Bill became my go-to guide for unlocking the secrets of the Sonoran Desert. He shared extensive knowledge about the caves, intricate geology, and unique features of the Sonoran Desert landscape. We went on explorations together, and the trips to Kartchner Caverns and Colossal Caves were standout, unforgettable highlights.

He was a treasure trove of adventure stories. One evening, we arranged to meet at Borderlands Brewery for a beer. Seated on the patio and enveloped by the lively atmosphere, we observed as the sun commenced its descent, casting a warm glow over our conversation. Occasionally, the passing train and its characteristic rumble interrupted our chat.

"So, what makes the saguaro such a unique plant?" I finally asked him about his favorite topic.

Taking a thoughtful sip of his beer, Bill began to explain, "It's the largest cactus on this side of the border, with greater concentrations here than in Mexico. But, more importantly, the saguaro has become the icon of the entire Sonoran Desert. Almost anywhere in the world, if you hold up your arm with an empty hand, that is a sign of peaceful greeting. This says, 'See, I have no weapons.' So, at some unconscious level, when we see saguaros with their upraised 'arms,' we see them as human figures and they inspire good feelings.

"This sign has been with humanity for such a long time; it seems to be recognized at an instinctual level for many cultures worldwide. Now it is also the main and certainly unique symbol of the Sonoran Desert. It is a really cool plant too, as long as you don't touch it!"

"Very interesting! I hadn't thought about it this way," I continued, "So, does it play an important role in the Sonoran Desert?"

Bill nodded, "Yes. There are more animals associated with the saguaro than anything else in the Sonoran Desert. And, that's one of the ways we know that it has been here a long time. It's only in the last couple of years, with DNA, that we figured out it has been here for several million years: longer than everything else except the rocks it lives on.

"The great length of time that the saguaro has existed has enabled it to form numerous relationships with animals. Birds make their homes in it and utilize it for various purposes. Many of them hunt insects around the flowers and also find nourishment in its nectar and fruit. Similarly, ground-dwelling animals may seek shade and shelter within its structure. Additionally, Native Americans utilized the saguaro for food, tools, and building materials."

"What sets it apart from other cacti?"

Bill continued to enlighten me, "For a succulent cactus, they grow to be very big, and the growth is slow. They can wait out the bad times and bad weather conditions because they live such a long time. These cacti can grow to be huge to store food and water. So, they can escape a lot of problems that a shorter-lived or smaller plant would face in such a harsh environment. Yet they only have to produce one surviving seed.

"The larger saguaros may live to be 175 years old or more. So, if they only need to have one good year in 175 years, that is a major advantage for them. They may live a shorter time, but there is that opportunity in the population for them to live a lot longer. That 175 years is an average. When they are growing in the low desert, where conditions are harsher, they grow even more slowly. While most desert plants grow slowly for various reasons, they don't have long lifespans like saguaros. They are experts in survival."

"That's incredible! So, what makes the Sonoran Desert the greenest desert in the world?"

"Our annual summer monsoon brings a second rainy season. Winters are cooler, summers much warmer, and we experience rain in both periods. This unique climate allows for a diverse array of plant species, including cacti that may have evolved right here. Interestingly, many desert plants originated elsewhere and migrated to this region. Many of them have ancestors from the south which is tropical, but they found that they can live here or were stranded here during earlier changes in the climate. They have adapted to the two rain cycles.

"We have plants that go dormant during the winter, and then when the heat and warmth come back, they thrive. Some of these desert plants would not be able to take the cold unless they had adapted to drop their leaves in the winter. That may also be part of the reason why we have more species than other deserts. Also, you need to consider the opportunities for many more kinds of plants provided by the great range of the elevations of the Sky Island Mountains and the latitudinal extent of the Sonoran Desert.

"So most states in the US will have 2000 to 2500 species of plants; Arizona has over 3500 species. This applies as well to the animal kingdom. The result is much less biomass but much greater diversity. Take this and add in effects of great numbers of people only for the past few hundred years and that makes the Sonoran Desert the last one in the world to be heavily impacted by humans."

Captivated by his geological wisdom, I asked, "How is it possible that the city is surrounded by so many mountains?"

Bill paused and grinned, "It's because we're on the edge of the continent. For hundreds of millions of years, Arizona has been drifting north. At one point, we were actually south of the equator. Being on the corner of a moving tectonic plate is part of the effect. All plates contact their neighbors, but when you're on a corner, you can be affected no matter which way you or your neighbor moves. The crust of the earth contains records of these events, from repeated collisions to casual scrapes."

He paused, and then continued, "Earlier in this area, moving east to west, the North American plate slid over the Pacific plate causing the mountain ranges and volcanoes of the Rocky Mountains to build up the terrain. But then more recently, to our west, crustal material from the south began to move northward to collide with the western edge of our plate.

"As a passing foot can wrinkle and twist a throw rug, the local crust of this area was deformed by stretching and fracturing to form the valley and mountain terrains during what we now call the Basin and Range event. The Tucson Basin was created in this manner by its 'sinking' relative to the mountains that surround it. In geological terms, this happened so fast that large portions of the over-steepened mountain slopes cascaded into the deepening valley as it formed in a series of slow-motion mega-landslides.

"The Tucson Mountains located to the west of downtown Tucson, is our best example of this process. There, the mountains that you see have no 'roots' at 760m/ 2500ft below the present surface. They were cut off from their original location above the southwestern tops of the Catalina Mountains to the NE of downtown Tucson and slid down a 20-degree slope to come to rest in their present position. This relationship was only confirmed in the early 1990s, and helps to explain many of the strange and wonderful close associations of very different types of rocks and minerals that can be found in the Tucson area."

As Bill shared his stories, he used beer mats as makeshift tectonic plates to illustrate geological movements. It turned into a delightful lesson in geology over beers. With the occasional passing train adding its rumble, we decided to call it a night.

Brushstrokes & Lassos: Famous Artists & Dude Ranching

with Domingo DeGrazia, Diana Madaras, and Russell True

Bob and Molly returned from their travels, sparking a fresh sense of exploration that filled our days. Our conversations, inspired by the rich hues of the desert, dived into the intricacies of color, patterns, and art. We decided to visit Ted DeGrazia's Gallery in the Sun, an artistic sanctuary that also provides a peaceful retreat surrounded by natural beauty.

Molly, with her usual enthusiasm, shared the intriguing history of the gallery. She described how the late Ted DeGrazia, a local artist, envisioned and built it as a studio, home, and gallery to showcase his art. Nestled against the backdrop of the Santa Catalina mountains, the complex featured several adobe-style buildings with earthy tones, rounded edges, and rustic detailing.

Exploring the gallery and spending time in the garden became my cherished activities. Ted's collection of paintings vividly depicted the local cultural history.

Our excitement peaked upon discovering the upcoming fiesta in honor of DeGrazia's birthday. The promise of festivities, complete with live music added an extra layer of anticipation to our explorations.

Fate, always a silent companion in my adventures, intervened when I unexpectedly met Lance, the current gallery director. During our conversation, I mentioned my book project. Generously, Lance provided me with contact information for Ted's youngest son,

Domingo. We arranged a coffee meeting, promising to unfold another chapter of my Tucson journey into art.

—

Domingo DeGrazia is the youngest son of renowned artist Ettore "Ted" DeGrazia. He graduated from Embry-Riddle Aeronautical University and earned his law degree from Oklahoma City University, practicing as a trial attorney in the juvenile court system. In addition to his legal pursuits, Domingo is a respected guitarist and songwriter, blending Spanish, Latin, and Flamenco styles. Furthermore, he has actively contributed to the political landscape, serving as a Democratic member of the Arizona House of Representatives from 2019 to 2023, representing District 10.

—

Meeting Domingo was truly delightful. We chose a shaded patio at Hotel Congress, which radiated the ambiance of an old traditional hotel with historic charm. It was late morning, and just a few people were sitting outside, creating a serene and relaxed atmosphere.

Domingo is one of those inconspicuous people you might not notice at first, but he has a lot of interests and talents hidden within, making him a renaissance man. Domingo was not only very sincere and modest but also appreciative.

"Thank you for what you are doing," he said after I briefly told him about my intention to culturally capture Tucson.

As we sipped our coffee, I pressed the record button, eager to hear more about his experiences and memories. Firstly I wanted to know more about his dad.

"What are your memories of your dad?" I began.

Domingo responded without hesitation: "He passed when I was eight. I didn't have much time to know him because he was not married to my mom when I was born. His wife at a time was Marien, making me essentially illegitimate.

"So, I didn't live with him at the gallery. But I think that in some ways, that might have helped me. I did not have a lot of time with

48

him before he passed, which kept me out of the spotlight and the pressure of being like him. Growing up, I wanted him to be proud of me, but I didn't have the same kind of pressure that others might have."

He paused and I did not say anything, providing him space to continue.

"I feel like I spent most of my childhood in the backseat of a Suburban, as we visited almost every Pow wow or ceremony taking place throughout Arizona. That's probably why I don't like driving. I do remember some of the Pow wows and Sunrise Dances up at the Navajo and Hopi reservations, and I was an eagle dancer for a while, so I would wear eagle feathers and perform at some places.

"With my dad, we spent a lot of time in the Superstition Mountains panning for gold. We also explored many rivers, the Salt River among them, learning how to work with a pan. Those are very fond memories I have—spending time with him, doing that.

"It's been an amazing journey learning about him through the people who knew him. Even today, people approach me, knowing he's my dad, sharing vibrant and vivid memories. He had that kind of impact on people, that 30 years later they still remember exactly how it happened and are really excited to share the story. So, his memory remains very present in many lives."

"That's fascinating. Why do you think he spent so much time with Native Americans?"

Domingo took a sip of his coffee and continued: "I am guessing because it was a culture similar to what he would've had in Italy – small towns recognizing the value and importance of the people on the land, the miners, and the workers. He was so prolific, always making art with everything he found, like soda pop cans, which aligned with Native American culture's use of everyday materials.

"Tribal members and Hispanics were his circle of friends, so it was a lifestyle, a lot of Native American dances and other rituals, and you can see it throughout his paintings."

I followed up, "What were his biggest milestones?"

"There were probably a few milestones, considering his growth as an artist and then his ability to showcase his art to the world. I believe a significant moment was when he was 33 years old and in Mexico, meeting with Diego Rivera, Mexico's master muralist. During WWII Rivera wrote a letter to the U.S. government, essentially saying not to enlist him in the US military because he was destined to become a great American artist.

"This support from such an influential artist is substantial for any artist. During this period, they collaborated on murals, marking Ted's darker phase, where some of his art carried communist ideas. Upon returning to Tucson, he resumed immersion in the environment of Native Americans and Mexicans, which became his primary theme and the longest period showcased in the gallery.

"Another big milestone occurred in 1960 when UNICEF requested permission to use his image of Los Niños—children dancing in a circle—to produce greeting cards. This made him the most reproduced artist at that time, and through a long-term collaboration with Arizona Highways Magazine, he gained worldwide exposure.

"This prominence within the artist community and the perception of what a southwestern artist should be provided momentum for him to explore other things with a bit less pressure. And of course, completing the gallery in 1965 and being able to show his art was also a very important milestone.

"So, he goes from painting with watercolors and oils, murals, jewelry, textiles, stone lithographs, and serigraphs, to the construction of the building. I think it is a really magical part of his life, where everything came together. And you can see it and touch it."

"Did he face any setbacks?" I continued.

"Oh, absolutely. That's part of the journey. Ted was a vibrant and sometimes controversial individual. I remember a story that happened when he was around 32 years old, keen to sell his artwork and gain more recognition.

"One night, feeling frustrated and perhaps after a few drinks, he decided to put some of his artwork on the sidewalk outside his gallery on Campbell.

"He wanted people to take it for free, a kind of impromptu art giveaway. He passed out and woke up the next morning only to find all the artwork still there! Not a single piece was taken. For an artist, that could be devastating.

"However, shortly after that, he got featured in Arizona Highways. Life has a way of surprising you."

"How has your life been influenced by his art?"

"I do paint, and I'm terrible at it. It came down to guitar for me. I'm told I have some musical talent, but I don't think that's true because I know how many hours I put into practice and rehearsal. I see it more as hard work, but there's something within me that allowed me to stay with music and keep going back to it throughout my life.

"If there is any talent, it's just the persistence to stick with it because that's what my dad said, 'When you become a famous artist, it's when your beard grows white.' I think what he meant was just, when you have done it for decades—not months, not years, but literary decades—that's when you become a true artist."

"Yes, but that can be challenging at times, no?"

"Yes, I agree. For me, if the artist is happy and everything is perfect, then the art doesn't come out right. You have to have a little bit of unhappiness, an internal struggle to make the true story come through. That's what I find in my music."

After bidding farewell to Domingo, I felt the need to ponder on his words. Taking a stroll, I contemplated the profound insights he shared.

When I recounted the story to Bob and Molly, they were delighted with my encounter. Molly chimed in, "Do you know Linda Ronstadt? She was a big rock star! You should talk to her!"

Fascinated, we decided to explore Linda Ronstadt's world by watching a documentary about her that evening—it was a remarkable movie. However, my hopes of meeting her were dampened when I discovered that she had relocated to California.

"Ah, she's too far away. That's not gonna happen," I remarked. Unwilling to entirely let go of my wish, I added, "Maybe it will happen in a different way; I'll put my wish out to the universe."

—

Molly, being the enthusiast she was, decided to organize a small house party. As we planned the gathering for some of their friends and people from around the neighborhood, I noticed Diana Madaras on the guest list. Another brilliant local artist! I was looking forward to meeting her.

The connections and opportunities unfolding in Tucson continued to amaze me. It turned out to be a very inspiring evening. And yes, you can't miss Diana in a room. She emanates strong and magnetic energy, drawing everyone's attention effortlessly.

As our conversation unfolded, I was pleasantly surprised to discover Diana's deep love and care for animals, a passion that added another layer to her already sophisticated personality. Upon sharing my idea for a book, she generously extended an invitation to her house for an interview.

—

Diana Madaras earned a master's degree in Bio-mechanics from the University of Arizona and spent 18 years in a high-profile sports marketing company in Tucson, where she promoted major sporting events such as LPGA and PGA golf tournaments. In 1996, she sold her marketing company to pursue a career as a professional artist. Throughout her artistic journey, Diana has received numerous accolades, including being voted Tucson's Best Visual Artist nine times, being recognized as philanthropist of the year, and receiving the prestigious Wells Fargo Copper Cactus Award—an esteemed honor in Tucson for community service.

—

Surprisingly, Diana lived just a stone's throw away. Two dogs warmly welcomed me as I entered, and the air was filled with the vibrant energy of creativity. Diana's home was a testament to her artistic talent, walls embellished with her art.

She poured a cup of coffee, and we took a seat at her round dining table, admiring one of her art pieces—a large-scale painting portraying violet mountains and a pink sky.

Recalling that Diana had mentioned owning a company and being in the sports marketing business for a long time, I was curious how someone could change careers at such a late stage.

"What impulse led you to sell your company and become a painter?"

She paused, deep in thought, and then shared... "I had painted during high school but had to stop due to my professional career. However, during a vacation in the Bahamas in 1992, I came across another artist's painting that reignited my passion and inspired me to start again.

"A year later, during my time at the University of Arizona, a professor named Chuck Albanese saw my work and encouraged me to join his group for a month-long painting course in Greece. That trip changed my life, immersing me in a world of colors and altering my perspective. Once I stepped out of my comfort zone, there was no turning back. My life became a canvas of colors, and I was truly altered by the experience. Upon returning, I dedicated myself to painting as much as possible.

"Soon thereafter, I displayed some of my own and Chuck's paintings in a building I owned on Broadway, thus opening my first small gallery. It was at that moment I realized that pursuing art as a profession was a viable option. Over the next couple of years, we began selling paintings on a larger scale.

"Eventually, I made the decision to sell my company and transitioned to painting full-time. It was an instinctive choice driven by a strong inner pull; it wasn't a matter of choice but rather the only thing I wanted to do."

Engaging in our conversation, I delved into her artwork, noting the collection of spirit animals and wildlife. I asked,

"What do these paintings mean to you?"

"Growing up in my dad's veterinary hospital, my love for animals has been ingrained in me since childhood. This connection led to establishing a foundation to help abused, injured, and homeless animals.

"A few years ago, I had the privilege of representing an artist named John Nieto, renowned for his vibrant and colorful depictions of coyotes and wolves. His work, inspiring me, now graces my gallery. Spirit animals and wildlife art hold profound meanings beyond their aesthetic beauty; they symbolize a deep connection to the rich spirit of this region."

I was intrigued to know more about her philanthropic endeavors, so I asked, "Your organization, Art for Animals, is involved in many projects. Which one brings you the greatest joy?"

"Mostly, the Tucson Wildlife Center. There used to be twelve Wildlife Rescue Centers in Southern Arizona, and now there is one. So, it was really important to save that one. I have dedicated my efforts during the last decade to help them. They save the lives of more than 5000 animals yearly and cover 8 counties. They help the whole gambit of wildlife: coyotes, javelinas, mountain lions, raptors, little quail.

"Most of the injuries are caused by humans. The animals often are either hit by cars or poisoned. For instance, when people poison rats, birds eat them and fall ill. Also, construction sites contribute to habitat destruction. Many of these challenges arise from harmful human activities. We have the responsibility to take care of these poor native animals, because not only do we encroach on their environment, but also we contribute significantly to their suffering."

"Where do you find your greatest inspiration here in Tucson?"

"I find my greatest inspiration by observing the interplay of sunlight and shadow. The captivating combination of light and shadow creates intriguing shapes, forms, and scenes. I always carry my camera with me to capture these moments, serving as an inspiration in my studio.

"Exploring the diverse and ever-changing desert landscapes, with mountains undergoing captivating color transformations and prickly pear cacti changing hues, brings me joy. The abundance of wildlife and the rich Western influence in this region are additional sources of inspiration that I deeply cherish."

"What makes Tucson such a unique city?"

"The culture. The landscape. The people. There is a real connection to the Earth here, with a lot of ancient history from Native American and Mexican cultures. They have influenced the architecture, food, language, and arts communities. You see it everywhere you look. As a painter, I love the clear sky and warm colors. Sunsets here are so saturated with color that they seem almost unreal.

"The sky in Tucson turns pink due to the sunlight's interaction with the atmosphere. When the sun is low in the sky during sunrise or sunset, its light has to pass through more of the air. This causes the shorter blue and green wavelengths to scatter more, while the longer red and pink wavelengths linger, imparting a pinkish hue to the sky. The spectacle is truly beautiful, especially with Tucson's mountains and desert scenery enhancing the colorful display."

To my astonishment, she gifted me her biography, a gorgeous coffee table book. Then in her typical straightforward manner, she said out of the blue, "Do you know Russell True? He owns the White Stallion Ranch."

"No," I replied.

"You should talk to him, he is my friend," she added, handing me his contact information.

—

Russell True is the owner of the White Stallion Ranch, Tombstone Monument Ranch, and Rancho de La Osa. He co-founded and served as a president of the Arizona Dude Ranch Association and two-time president of the national Dude Ranchers' Association. Among many roles on the ranch, he is manager, saddler, wrangler, cook, and a great storyteller.

—

Arriving at the White Stallion Ranch felt like stepping into a time machine, transporting me back to the last century in the heart of the Wild West. The air resonated with the sounds of horses' whinnies, the rhythmic beat of hooves, and the sight of cowboys going about their business, all against the backdrop of the breathtaking natural beauty at the north end of the Tucson Mountains.

Eager to immerse myself in this atmosphere, I took a leisurely stroll around the magnificent ranch, taking in the sights and sounds of an Old Pueblo era. Afterwards, I made my way to the reception area, where I awaited my meeting with Russell.

Russell, a hands-on leader, caught my attention as he dedicatedly oversaw every aspect of the ranch. More than a businessman, he appeared to be the heart and soul of the operation—a skilled chef, a caring host, and a true steward of the Western experience. His commitment to the ranch extended beyond mere business interests.

Over lunch, my fascination with dude ranching deepened as Russell generously shared insights into the unique world of ranch life. The experience was not just a meal but a journey into the heart of Western hospitality, where stories of cowboy traditions, horse-manship, and the spirit of the Wild West unfolded. The more we talked, the more I realized the profound connection between the ranch and its surroundings, making me avid to explore and understand this authentic slice of Western culture.

"What is dude ranching and how did it start?" I couldn't help but ask.

Russell reflected briefly before sharing the history: "A dude ranch is essentially a rural cattle ranch that welcomes tourists. Some are more like resorts, while others are basic cattle ranches with fewer guests. Traditionally, they accommodate 30 to 40 guests for activities like riding, eating, sleeping, hiking, and socializing. The concept began in the Dakota territories when former President Teddy Roosevelt invited wealthy friends from the East Coast to his cattle ranch. In 1892, it was officially recognized as hospitality. The guests were called dudes because they came from the East all duded up."

"So, why is dude ranching so important for Tucson's history?"

"Tucson, truly, and pretty unarguably, was the dude ranch capital of the world. There was a research project done by graduate student Frank Norris who found 137 dude ranches in the Tucson area, not counting outliers. It probably peaked in the 40's and 50's as Tucson grew. However, like many western cities in the 60's, ranches got sold or paved over. When we arrived in 1965, there were still 24 dude ranches in Tucson. People like my father were major players in the tourism industry because dude ranches still brought in a lot of wealthy tourists from other states. They were really respected and an important part of the city tourism and culture."

"Why did so many people keep coming here back then? Why was it so popular to travel that far?"

"The weather and the wildness. Hollywood movies significantly contributed to the popularity of this area, where cowboys embodied the image of the west. And that image was shaped as Westerns portrayed cowboys as white-hat-wearing, damsel-saving, ethical giants.

"But before the movies, it was the frontier. It was the wilderness, the animals, the nature, the vastness. Then, as Westerns exploded across America, gas was thrown on the flames. Nowadays, people grow up on Star Wars, superheroes, not John Wayne. Young people don't even know why Tombstone is interesting, or why it's the most iconic western town. But I think everything circles back to our natural setting. The expanses, the opportunities, still are such a big contrast from most urban lives."

"So what were the real cowboys like?"

"A real cowboy was and still is a person who works on a ranch. It is not necessarily a flattering term. Cowboys in reality are people who might have some real skills, such as roping, branding, riding fence, scouting trail, finding water, managing cattle—just doing ranch stuff.

"But they can be rootless people who live from paycheck to paycheck. The cattlemen were always the people with property and respect. But that was too nuanced in a lot of ways for Hollywood and it would not have played that well. So they just put them all together and created a new image of a cowboy, who was living on a ranch, chasing cows, and taking care of women.

"The Hollywood version of the cowboy became the symbol of the West, and one of the very unique things about America."

We had finished our lunch. Russell stood up, gesturing for me to follow. "Do you want to see it? I'll show you around the ranch."

"That would be great! How old is your ranch?" I asked as we were walking out.

"It has a 120 year-old history. The main dining room was built around 1900, and afterwards a well and corrals were put in. It changed hands a few times and was finally sold to my parents in 1965. They came from Colorado and were tired of snow and cold. They fell in love with Tucson, the culture, the weather, everything about the city. They did not know what to do, because they had sold their business.

"My dad talked my mother into buying White Stallion Ranch after which she said: 'If I can look at those mountains to the south every morning when I wake up, I will let you throw our lives away.' This is literally how we got started and we continue in that family tradition. For more than 55 years we have been doing what we do."

Exploring the casitas, private cinema, and outdoor horse corral was a moment that completely captivated me. The rustic charm of the casitas, the allure of the private cinema, and the lively energy around the horse corral painted a vivid picture of the authentic Wild West experience. Against the stunning Sonoran Desert landscape, witnessing sturdy horses added an extra layer of charm.

The experience was nothing short of incredible. After thanking Russell and watching him go about his work, I slowly made my way back to the car. The excitement of the encounter led me to a decision —I was going to dive into the world of horseback riding!

———

I started taking a few lessons and began exploring various ranches, trying out different riding options, and experiencing the views from a saddle at various times of the day. It turned into one of the most beautiful moments of my life. Each ride introduced me to different horses and their personalities, from the calm to the energetic, and offered breathtaking views that made the entire experience truly rewarding.

During this time, Bob and Molly set out on a three-week trip to Florida, leaving me to focus on my work and indulge in horseback riding whenever possible. This period brought a sense of stability, and my English continued to improve as the first pages of my book started to come together. However, as life often goes, just when I was savoring one of the happiest periods, things took an unexpected turn.

Descent into the Valley

When Bob and Molly returned from their trip to Florida, where they visited family, things felt different. They wanted to have a chat with me, and the tone was unusually serious. As we gathered in the living room, they revealed the somber news that one of their family members was dealing with a severe illness, requiring their immediate attention on the East Coast. Since they're both originally from the East Coast, they discussed the possibility of moving back to be with their family during this challenging time.

"I am sorry to hear that. I understand," I responded, trying to process the unexpected turn of events. Seeking reassurance, I asked, "So, when will this be happening?"

"Don't worry, it will take us a few months," brought a mix of relief and uncertainty. They generously added, "You are welcome to stay here until then." The ground beneath me felt a little shaky, but the assurance that the move wouldn't happen hastily offered some comfort. I felt grateful and decided to make the most out of the time ahead, focusing on getting as much done as possible in the coming months.

In the midst of the shifting dynamics with Bob and Molly's impending move, I found solace in my work commitments and stumbled upon a fascinating opportunity.

During my research, I discovered the Canelo Project, a small private property dedicated to natural materials and buildings, located far south from Tucson. While navigating their website, I discovered that they were planning an open-door visit in the near future. Enthralled by the prospect of exploring this unique space, I quickly signed up for the upcoming event.

This unforeseen development promised a refreshing diversion, providing me with a chance to immerse myself into a different subject and acquire some new knowledge and inspiration for my research.

—

In less than a week, I found myself behind the wheel, heading southward to Sonoita. The winding roads through the beautiful rolling grasslands of Las Cienegas offered a captivating change of scenery.

As I arrived at the ranch, I parked my car and walked toward someone who was waving at me from a distance. Together, we walked inside.

It was a small, cozy gathering of six guests convened in the warm and inviting kitchen of a uniquely colorful adobe house. The rounded corners and earthen textures gave the space a warm and inviting feel, instantly putting us at ease. Our gracious hosts, Athena and Bill Steen, not only opened their home but also shared their extensive knowledge and passion for working with clay and straw-bale buildings.

The tour began in the kitchen, where Athena and Bill showcased a range of clay-based creations, demonstrating the versatility and beauty of this natural material. The vibrant colors and organic shapes of the adobe structures blended seamlessly with the surrounding landscape, creating a harmonious and aesthetically pleasing environment.

As we toured the house, Athena and Bill generously shared insights into the construction techniques and sustainable practices they employed. The walls, adorned with artwork and intricate clay designs, reflected the artistic spirit that infused the entire space.

Every room seemed to narrate a story of creativity, craftsmanship, and a deep connection to the earth. The combination of various colors, which initially seemed like an unlikely fit, came together harmoniously, creating a vibrant and lively environment, reminiscent of the dynamic Mexican aesthetic.

The tour extended beyond the house, venturing into the extensive property where Athena and Bill presented larger-scale projects. This included different straw-bale structures, an outdoor kitchen with a clay oven, and numerous examples showing a spectrum of clay colors.

It was an incredibly inspiring day, culminating in a gathering marked by free-flowing conversations. In the midst of our chat, I shared with Bill my intention to write a book about Tucson. To my surprise, his response opened unexpected doors for me, "You should definitely include the Ronstadts."

"Yes, you are right! I would like to, but Linda lives in California," I replied.

Bill then mentioned Petie, a musician and Linda's nephew, suggesting, "He's my friend. I'll share his contact. He lives in Tucson!"

A serendipitous connection was made, marking the beginning of my meeting with Peter Ronstadt, a significant chapter in my exploration of Tucson's vibrant musical scene and historical background.

Desert Rhythms: The Ronstadts, Mariachi & Echoes of Tucson's Heritage

with Peter Dalton Ronstadt, Daniel Buckley, and Jim Turner

—

Peter Dalton Ronstadt, also known as Petie, is a fifth-generation Tucsonan Ronstadt. He is a great-grandson of Federico José María Ronstadt, mover and shaker of early Tucson, and a nephew of Linda Ronstadt, the famous Rock 'n' Roller. Peter is a versatile musician, proficient in playing the bass, guitar, banjo, tuba, and singing. Beyond his musical talents, he is a writer and interpreter of songs, a recording engineer and producer, as well as a poet and lyricist.

—

Our paths first crossed at Petie's music studio, where the welcoming ambiance, complemented by his friendly and humble demeanor, created a delightful encounter.

As I shared fragments of my story and the reasons behind my book, my curiosity about Petie's family history grew.

"Tell me about your great-grandfather's story," I inquired, and with genuine enthusiasm, he began recounting the captivating narrative: "Federico came in the late 1800s as a young man. His father, who had migrated from Germany to Mexico, brought him north to Tucson to learn the trade of blacksmithing. Their arrival coincided with the time when the railroad was making its way to Tucson, a period of significant western expansion.

"He became a blacksmith and later applied his knowledge to be a wheelwright and a wagon maker. His establishment, known as The F.

Ronstadt Company, specialized in crafting wagons and carriages. Over time, it evolved into a comprehensive hardware store; as my dad would say, they sold everything from tractors to teaspoons. It became a hub where a diverse array of people gathered."

"Wow, that was a really exciting time… So, how did he become a great musician and a public personality?"

"Before coming to Tucson, he studied music at the University of Sonora. During that time, there was no organized music and culture in Tucson. So, he created the first philharmonic 20-piece band in Tucson and named it Club Filarmónico Tucsonense.

"He personally taught most of the musicians how to play their instruments because not many of them knew what they were doing before that. Being the only band in town, they became the go-to ensemble, performing at various social occasions including funerals, weddings, dances, and *quinceañeras*, covering every social gathering at that time.

"His hardware store, now replaced by a bus station, remained open in Tucson for 97 years before closing down. He became a prominent Tucsonan, firmly rooted in the city's establishment. Despite people wanting him to get involved in politics, he refused. However, he played a significant role in various aspects of Tucson life at the time, contributing to musical culture, the founding of the Desert Museum, and assisting in creating the iconic 'A' on 'A' Mountain. As Tucson was developing its identity, he played a vital role in shaping it, but his true passion always remained music."

"How did Tucson look when he first came? What was preserved until now?"

"In the late 1800s, Tucson evolved into a railroad town, giving rise to a cadre of skilled architects who played a pivotal role in shaping the city's distinctive appearance. This period, characterized by architects like Josias Joesler, Roy Place, and many houses in the Sam Hughes neighborhood, represents the quintessence of Tucson's architectural identity to me. It's a fusion of *hacienda* architecture from

Northern Mexico, the New Spanish Colonial style of California, hints of Moorish influence, and a touch of Santa Fe aesthetics—a unique blend that defines Tucson for me. These architects skillfully blended various styles, creating structures that still resonate with the spirit of Tucson. Beyond architecture, Tucson reflects this blending in its people.

"In a world often characterized by division, Tucson stands out as a place where individuals actively seek to immerse themselves in diverse cultures and identities, enhancing the richness of their own lives. And I think that's kind of the beauty of Tucson."

"That's remarkable." I was stunned by the idea of Tucson's harmonious blend, and continued, "So, what was it like growing up in such a musical family? And especially with your Aunt Linda?"

"Linda was always a very supportive and close aunt throughout my entire childhood. She was just my aunt, despite being around people that everyone else would be star-struck by. When I was a kid, George Lucas, who she was dating, was like an uncle to me. I loved Star Wars movies, but I did not connect that he was the guy who created the Star Wars universe."

"Amazing!" We both were laughing.

"I mean, I knew that they were his movies, but they were not mega-stars for me, and I did not realize that she was a star. It was not until my mid to late 20's when I came out of punk rock and Indie rock into the world of acoustic and traditional music. As I started listening more to Linda's records, I suddenly saw her in a new light.

"That aunt, with whom I've always goofed around, is an icon! Moreover, much of what she created resonated with what we did during our family gatherings—breaking barriers in various genres. She was doing country, pop, rock, R&B, sometimes on the same record. That was not a weird thing for us. In our living room during family gatherings, all kinds of music played. We'd get together, make some food, tell stories, and play music. When I was younger,

I thought that's what all families do. Now I know that it was very special within the Ronstadt family and has persisted for generations."

"Could you describe the style of music you play in more detail?"

"I like to say that we play what I call 'living room music,' presenting it in different venues. You could call it Americana, but we also perform Mexican songs. We refer to it as the Postmodern American West, a term coined by Bill Steen. Essentially, it encompasses a little bit of everything. Here in Tucson, I collaborate with a group of musicians that I call 'The Company.' I throw whatever is on my mind at them, and they are a gracious group, allowing me to take them wherever I want to go.

"That means we could be singing an old Mexican ballad with minimal instrumentation and closed vocal harmonies, followed by a Muddy Waters tune that's raw and gritty, and then transition to some original music. We really mix it up. In addition to 'The Company,' I've been putting a lot of effort into a singing duo simply called Liz & Pete. It's been a new and enjoyable adventure. Singing with a non-relative has been a rewarding challenge and a new direction for the music. And when things line up just right, we get to have everyone on the same stage together."

"In which venues do you play? And what sort of live music is in town?"

"In this town, you'll always find a diverse range of genres, including country, rock, Americana, and Mexican music, as well as mariachi, folk, jazz, classical, R&B, and delightful combinations of these styles. The bar scene, both indoors and outdoors, is lively.

"I have a regular gig at Monterey Court, and I also perform solo in various spots across town. Some other fantastic venues to explore include the Rialto, Fox Theatre, and Hotel Congress. Personally, I have a soft spot for the Temple of Music and Art, an absolutely spectacular building.

"Tucson boasts numerous venues, breweries, and hotels that showcase both local talents and international musicians, creating a beautiful fusion that perfectly complements the city's vibrant and diverse cultural scene."

"What does Tucson sound like to you?"

"I wrote a line in one of my songs." He paused. "Do you listen to any mariachi music?"

"Not much."

"So, there is a sound in the musical group Calexico that uses mariachi. There is a particular sound in mariachi music with two trumpets that harmonize in parallel lines together, and Calexico effectively incorporates them into a kind of folky, Indie rock. To me, there is something about those sounds that describes the vastness of the landscape, the colors of the sunset, and the purple of the mountains.

"It is an almost intoxicating beauty about this valley. The sound of those two trumpets and mariachi playing these parallel lines can truly evoke the imagery of the landscape for me because those sounds are among my earliest memories. I wrote a song when I was coming back west from the East Coast. It's about coming back to the valley. I was traveling a lot, but I realized this is the place for me to come back home."

I was silent. Then he continued, "People have apparently been settling and congregating in this valley for much longer than we can record in history; artifacts have been found, so there's got to be something about this place..."

And then he found and played his song called The Horse and the Barn.

69

The Horse and The Barn - Peter Dalton Ronstadt

These tear soaked lands of rain and fog I'll leave behind,
For the quiet of that valley embathed in sweet sunshine.
The valley of my people and the ones who came before,
When the river ran so deeply we could ride her to the shore.

Whoa, Whoa, aah, aah

Lupe wrote of shaking earth and rocks falling' round,
There was changing of the rivers and we forced that table down.
We've taken it for granted that our valley will give freely,
To all who call on her except for those who truly see.

Yet she sits there in the distance calling me to come back home,
No I cannot give resistance, it's the only home I know.

I, know, aah, know, aah

The sun is rising fast and we ain't gonna last,
These hopeless deserts that we're wandering have but one thing to give back.
The dusty road I know is fading in the sand,
Will we be lost unto the hours or find our way to western lands?

The calling of the trumpets in the distance I can hear
them sweetly singing songs of freedom, songs of nectar to my ears

Aah, aah

Whoa, We ain't gonna last,

Aah, there's one thing to give back.

Whoa, In the distance I can hear,

Aah, Nectar to my ears.

Whoa, I'm leaving you behind,

Aah, For that sweet sunshine.

There are mountains in the distance and a valley I can see,

Now her loving saturation is washing over me.

Aah, aah

We fell into silence; no words were needed. This beautiful song marked the end of our conversation. I thanked him for his time, and we bid our goodbyes. It was such a pleasure to meet him.

With the rhythms of the valley still resonating in my mind, I drove back to the foothills, feeling content and excited about our encounter.

Upon my return, a realtor was just leaving, marking the official listing of the house. Bob and Molly reassured me, saying, "Don't worry. It's going to take a few months for sure," but the shift in energy was palpable. Despite their comforting words, I found it challenging to focus and tried to make the best use of my time.

—

In the days that followed, life graced me with yet another extraordinary encounter, this time with the self-proclaimed 'renaissance dude,' Dan Buckley. Our paths crossed at a Sunday brunch organized by Laura, where I was invited by a friend.

We exchanged numbers, and later on, we decided on Time Market, a restaurant and coffee shop near the U of A campus, as our rendez-vous point. The air was infused with the tantalizing scent of freshly baked pastries and pizza, perfectly harmonizing with the lively cadence of animated conversations.

Dan, also an avid mariachi enthusiast, not only shared his passion for this vibrant musical tradition but delved into the rich history that intertwines with Linda Ronstadt's illustrious career. Our conversation evolved into a delightful journey through the cultural scene of Tucson, woven with anecdotes about local music venues and the unique contributions of the mariachi scene. This unexpected connection left me inspired and grateful for the diverse and enriching encounters life continued to unfold in Tucson.

—

Daniel Buckley arrived in Arizona in 1971 to study lunar and planetary geology at the University of Arizona. Renowned for his roles as a journalist, music writer, historian, and documentary maker, he is also an accomplished photographer, videographer, composer, performance artist and sound designer. Buckley's multidisciplinary work earned him the recognition of Artist of the Year at the 2014 Arizona Governor's Arts Awards.

—

Dan revealed himself as a true polymath, engaged in various pursuits, but I could see his eyes consistently lit up at the mere mention of the word "mariachi." Seated by the expansive window, we observed the ebb and flow of people passing by. I couldn't resist delving into the heart of my curiosity, prompting the question, "What is mariachi?"

And Dan began to explain, "Mariachi or mariachis were originally musicians who would come to your house and play. A traditional mariachi group was composed of instruments from colonial Spain, eventually settling to violins, *vihuela*, guitar, vocals, and the harp. The harp was the major player. Once they started strolling and moving from house to house, it changed because you could not stroll with the harp, so they replaced the harp with the giant bass guitar, the *guitarrón*."

"How has mariachi evolved over time?"

"The trumpet was not originally a part of mariachi until the 1930s, the age of cinema and the radio. Microphones at the time couldn't capture the sound of the violin, so an engineer suggested hiring a trumpet player, placing them at a distance, and having them play the same line as the violins. It initially outraged listeners, and people called the radio station in horror. However, it has now become a defining instrument in the mariachi sound.

"But those were not the only changes. Mariachi was an all-male tradition, and women were not allowed to perform. That has also changed over time."

"What is the history of mariachi here in Tucson?"

"The first youth group in Tucson was Mariachi Los Changuitos Feos, which means 'ugly little monkeys.' After 16 years, a second mariachi group, Mariachi Nuevo, was introduced, and they included women. The problem always had been that boys did not want to play violins because of peer pressure. And then in the 60s and 70s, that macho culture was a bit of a block. But when women started coming, Tucson went from one group to two groups, and then many in rapid fashion. And now there are 40 or more, including all-female groups or mixed groups.

"A convergence of factors, including the launch of the Tucson International Mariachi Conference in 1983 and the implementation of guitar and mariachi programs in elementary schools, has played a significant role. Children begin their mariachi journey as early as kindergarten and can reach professional levels by the time they reach high school age!

"These young musicians not only embrace their cultural heritage but also become torchbearers, carrying the rich history and culture to future generations. A similar narrative unfolds with *baile folklórico*, groups of dancers showcasing diverse regional dances from the states and regions of Mexico."

"That's incredible!" I was amazed.

"It truly is," Dan nodded and continued, "In the 60s, far more Mexican Americans in Tucson lived in poverty. Today the majority of Mexican Americans pursue higher education, and mariachi played a pivotal role in this transformation, reshaping the whole economy. Our mayor, Regina Romero, is a mariachi mom. Pima County Supervisor Adelita Grijalva is also a mariachi mom, and Raúl Grijalva, our congressman, is a mariachi grandfather.

"There are many outstanding mariachi musicians originating from Tucson, marking a literal transformation and elevating the potential of the Mexican-American community astronomically."

"Very fascinating!" As I don't speak Spanish, I didn't understand what they were singing, so I asked, "What songs do mariachi sing, and why are they dressed up in these costumes?"

"The mariachi repertoire is a mix, having evolved into a very popular music genre. While its roots are in folk music, a significant portion of the repertoire remains true to those folk origins. However, one of the biggest leaps in legacy and sophistication happened through the famous Mariachi Vargas de Tecalitlán. In the late 1950s, they hired a classical musician, Ruben Fuentes, who began writing intricate and extraordinarily beautiful arrangements for the group. The legacy of Vargas is truly immense, with over 125 years of history. They rightfully claim the title of 'the best mariachi in the world,' and it's not an exaggeration.

"As for their distinctive costumes, they were influenced by the film industry, where mariachi musicians were portrayed as regal, dignified, and of the highest order. This led to the adoption of the *traje de charro*, the suit of the gentleman cowboy. These suits, along with the characteristic wide-brimmed hats, are reminiscent of what big, rich landowners in Mexico would wear. The hats have a unique design with a flip at the back, which acts like a spoiler on the back of a race car, providing stability when galloping on horseback, preventing the hat from flying away.

"Before this influence, mariachis simply wore what they had, but since then, the *traje de charro* has become a symbol of their identity, and it has remained a significant part of their tradition and attire up to the present day."

"Do you know why Linda Ronstadt started performing mariachi?"

"It was a lifelong dream for Linda but became a real possibility during the first Mariachi Conference here. At that time, Linda, who was already a big rockstar, came to see Lola Beltrán, who Ronstadt patterned her rock 'n' roll voice after. Linda's father called her and said, 'Linda, they are going to have this mariachi thing, and they are going to have Lola Beltrán sing.' He knew she had never seen Lola Beltrán perform live. So, Linda canceled touring and flew here to Tucson to see Lola Beltrán.

"At the beginning of the show, there were microphone issues causing them to squeal. Raul Aguirre, the MC, was trying to fill up time by introducing dignitaries and sponsors to the audience, including Linda's dad. He said, 'Ladies and gentlemen, this is Mr. Gilbert Ronstadt, owner of Ronstadt hardware shop here in town. You all know him, and you know he has a kind of famous daughter,

Linda,' and the spotlight shifted from Gilbert to Linda. When the crowd realized she was there, they started cheering!

"Meanwhile, Lola Beltrán was backstage and heard the crowd screaming, wondering why they were cheering when she hadn't even come out yet. They told her, 'Well, Linda Ronstadt is in the audience.' So Lola Beltrán replied, 'Fetch her.'

"They brought Linda backstage, and she was like a 5-year-old in front of Lola, expressing her love and admiration, saying she had been listening to her since she was a little girl. Linda shared that the rock stuff she does, she does it in that style. Lola replied, 'Yes, I know who you are.'

"Then, she turned to Ruben Fuentes, the arranger for Mariachi Vargas, and said, 'Ruben, help this young lady. She needs to record this music.' And that's literally how it got started."

"Wow, that's incredible! It's fascinating how chance encounters can lead to such significant moments in music history. So, where can I go to listen to mariachi here in town?"

"The best time is on the weekend. You can catch them at El Charro, Brother John's, Guadalajara Grill, Maria Bonita, La Chingada Cocina, American Eats, and many other places where they perform in a less formal setting. Another option is to attend church on Sundays at St. Augustine Cathedral."

We had a lot to discuss with Dan, but our time together came to an end, and we parted warmly.

—

Our home underwent a rapid transformation into a space filled with numerous boxes. Bob and Molly orchestrated the preparations for the move, welcoming potential buyers into our now bustling abode. The pace was swift, and the process incredibly seamless. They quickly found a buyer who not only accepted the asking price but also desired to move in within a mere three weeks.

The unexpected changes left me feeling stressed and unsure about the next steps. In a comforting and generous move, Bob offered to cover two months, a promise that eased some of the immediate concerns. Together, we explored a few short-term rental options.

Amidst the whirlwind of packing, I found myself boxing up my beloved books. As I placed them in cardboard confines, a sense of desperation washed over me. The realization hit hard – I might not have the time to read or finish them in this chaotic transition. As I sifted through history books, one local author's name caught my eye —Jim Turner. An idea sparked in me: perhaps I could reach out to him for insights into history and save some time. The prospect of gaining knowledge without diving into lengthy texts appealed to me, offering a glimmer of intellectual engagement amidst the upheaval of moving.

—

Jim Turner is a historian, author, editor and lecturer. Jim received his Masters degree in U.S. history from the University of Arizona in 1999. In 2001, he became the Outreach Historian for the Arizona Historical Society, collaborating with more than 60 regional museums. Before retiring in 2009, he co-authored a fourth grade textbook, The Arizona Story, and later wrote Arizona: A Celebration of the Grand Canyon State in 2011. Since 2009, Jim has been associated with Rio Nuevo Publishers and has authored four books for them. He also delivers entertaining history presentations for Arizona Humanities and various senior living communities in Tucson and Phoenix.

—

The next morning, I reached out to Jim and discovered that he lived not far from us. Despite the proximity, we opted to meet in the serene patio of La Cocina restaurant, very close to the Old Presidio in downtown Tucson.

There, I shared the story of my journey with Jim and made a bold request – could he condense the history of Tucson into a two-hour conversation? Jim chuckled at the ambitious ask and, true to his professional nature, began an almost unstoppable narrative. He was so supportive and wanted me to understand it as the true teacher he is.

"OK let's start from the early beginning. That goes back to at least 7000 B.C. and to the prehistoric cultures that lived here. They were mammoth hunters, and the climate was much different then. Jumping forward to about 300 A.D., we had the Hohokam prehistoric people (a name given to them by Pima[2] Indians, which means 'those who went before' or 'the ancient ones'). About 1300 AD they disappeared, most probably because of the 300 year drought. The Hohokam are famous in what is now the Tucson area for their early agricultural irrigation system and communal platform buildings."

"Fascinating...." I simply listened.

"Their relatives in the Phoenix Basin constructed a network of thousands of miles of irrigation canals, the second earliest canals in North America, which was a major ancient engineering achievement. Modern Native descendants in the Gila drainage are the Akimel O'odham (the River People); in the borderlands desert, the Tohono O'odham (the Desert People); and out by Yuma are the Hia C-eḍ O'odham (the Sand Dune People). They were all here when Jesuit missionary Father Eusebio Kino arrived in 1691."

"Who was Father Kino?"

"Father Kino, originally from Northern Italy, became a missionary after a healing experience. He prayed to Saint Francis Xavier for recovery, leading him to Northern Mexico and Arizona. Armed with degrees in mathematics, cartography, and theology, he devoted himself to missionary work. Compassionate and diplomatic, Kino saw his efforts as a service to the Indigenous people," explained Jim, shedding light on the historical figure.

"What happened when he came?"

---

[2] The term Pima was given to the Akimel O'odham (River People) by the Spanish colonists.

"He brought 500 cattle and taught the Indians how to be cowboys. The first cowboys in Arizona were Indians!

"In 1751, there was a revolt against the missionaries, and in 1752, the Spanish military built the presidio in Tubac. In 1775, Hugo O'Connor, an Irishman, working for the Spanish crown, decided to move the presidio forty miles north, to what is now downtown Tucson. There are several stories why he moved it, but one of the reasons was that there was already a big Indian village near Sentinel Peak in Indian words: S-cuk-Ṣon.

"In the Uto-Aztecan language spoken by the Indigenous people, that means, 'spring at the base of the black mountain', and the village was at the base of what we now call 'A' Mountain.

"It was near August 28th, Saint Augustine's Day, when Kino first held a Catholic mass at that village so he named the place San Agustin del S-cuk Ṣon. When the soldiers founded the fort east of the village 80 years later they named it El Presidio San Agustin del Tucson."

"What was the relationship between the local Indians, missionaries, and the Apaches?"

"The Apaches lived in the Rim Country to the north and east of Tucson and they were semi-nomadic. In the summertime, they lived in higher elevations, in a very nice climate with pine trees, and in the wintertime, they moved south to the Sierra Madre in Mexico, where it's warmer. Tucson was on their path, so they would come and raid for horses, food, and women. This is why there was a more harmonious relationship between Tohono O'odham and Spaniards because Apaches were their common enemy. The O'odham welcomed Europeans because they had food and they were their allies. The conflicts between O'odham and Apaches had been going for decades before the Spanish arrived and didn't end until Geronimo's final surrender in 1886."

"What were the biggest milestones that shaped the city to the present form? And what about the Gold Rush?"

"When Mexico won its war of independence in 1821, it changed its colonization policy from the military/missionary 'cross and sword' method to giving out large land grants to wealthy cattle ranchers.

"Although it happened hundreds of miles away the discovery of gold in California in 1848 made a major impact on Tucson's growth. Since Tucson was the only large town between El Paso, Texas, and San Diego, California, more than 10,000 prospectors passed through Tucson on their way to the gold fields. Many returned a few years later when gold was discovered near Yuma, and then Prescott.

"The next significant change was the Gadsden Purchase of 1854, when Tucson officially became part of the United States, although they didn't take possession or raise the first American flag until 1856. Tucson grew slowly but steadily for the next few decades, but the population exploded, and the demographics shifted when the railroad arrived in 1880.

"Once mining machinery could be shipped in by rail and ore shipped out, the copper industry boomed. New stores opened while merchants who had been in business for decades and packed in goods by mule train closed their doors or moved to mining communities away from the railroad lines. Mining and railroad professional men brought their families. Tucson's population was about 75% Hispanic before the railroad, and it dropped to 25% as the railroad brought Anglos and European immigrants looking for new opportunities on the Western frontier."

"What about the University of Arizona?"

"When the first 32 students entered the University of Arizona classrooms in Old Main in 1891, Tucson ceased to be a typical Wild West town. Two professors from Harvard and Stanford arrived and brought their wives. Artists arrived, and Tucson became a refined cultural oasis with poetry readings and chamber music recitals."

"It was changing so fast!"

"Yes, it was. The population continued to grow as health seekers and winter visitors stayed at the many sanitariums, resorts, and dude ranches in and around. Then, in the 1920s, tourism, now a mainstay of the city's economy, took off.

"Henry Ford made automobiles affordable and offered his employees two week paid vacations and other companies followed his lead. Auto camping became a craze and although many took Route 66 to Hollywood to see their favorite movie stars, others took Route 80, the 'Broadway of America,' which drove them through Tombstone and Tucson."

"What about the war time?"

"World War II was another milestone in Tucson's growth. The remote inland location and lots of sunshine made it perfect for air bases and pilot training fields. Plus lots of war production plants far away from the coasts where saboteurs might operate. After the war, many G.I.s who had been stationed here returned to go to college and bought homes with their veterans' benefits.

"The Cold War kept the war production plants open, and a relatively new invention, evaporative coolers (nicknamed swamp coolers), were very inexpensive compared to traditional ammonia-based air conditioning, making living in the desert Southwest quite tolerable."

"Why is Tucson called the Old Pueblo?"

"Bob Leatherwood was mayor of Tucson when the railroad arrived in 1880. He was so excited about it that he sent telegrams to officials in Los Angeles, Chicago, and New York.

"The telegram stated: 'His honor Bob Leatherwood, Mayor of Tucson, is pleased to announce that the ancient and honorable pueblo of Tucson is now connected with the civilized world.' He even sent one to the Pope in Rome. However, a witty telegraph operator down the line decided to send a reply: 'His Excellency, the Pope, is pleased to learn that the ancient and honorable Pueblo of Tucson is now connected to the civilized world, but begs to ask, where the hell is Tucson?'

"The town was called the ancient and honorable Pueblo for several decades and then in the 1920s, local tourism promoters decided 'The Old Pueblo' was catchier and would attract people looking for the Old West atmosphere."

Jim's insights were incredible! After two hours, I was worn out, but I was armed with newfound historical perspectives. Having him share the history of Tucson was like having a walking encyclopedia, and he made it fun and engaging.

Feeling grateful for the knowledge gained, I said my goodbyes and headed toward the foothills, mentally preparing for the upcoming move. This was a challenging time for me because everything in front of me was unknown.

—

As time passed, I found myself loading up my car with belongings. Molly surprised me with a box containing some of her jewelry and a few other thoughtful gifts. On that morning, we didn't see each other in person; she just sent a text, assuring me that we would meet again soon. Both of us were holding back tears, trying to stay composed. Bob gave me a tight hug, and I walked away from the house, as if it were any other day.

Glancing around, the place felt like a magical home that I was leaving behind, stepping into an unknown abyss without them. Tears streamed down my face as I drove down Mission Hill Drive into the valley, making it almost impossible to see the road ahead.

Abyss

I landed in an unfamiliar part of town, occupying a modest room with white walls situated on the west side of Ironwood Hills. The solitude in this foreign place evoked a disconcerting feeling.

As I lay on the bed, waves of uncertainty and stress washed over me, intensified by the absence of familiar faces. The room, furnished with only basic essentials—a plain built-in wardrobe, the bed beneath me, and a simple desk with a chair—underscored the challenges of navigating this new environment. It was a drastic change, and I was uncertain about what to do next.

Feeling desperate, I forced myself to start cleaning and unpacking, awaiting the evening as I reached out to Tereza.

"What should I do? I am unsure of what's expected of me now. It feels like my life just ended, and I don't hear any communication from my guides. Could you please give me a hint?"

"They are trying to get as much as possible out of you. You are undergoing tests of endurance and faith."

"Well, that's something," I thought.

"I can see that you are disconnected. You need to go to Nature. Nature will provide the stability you need. Reconnect with the land. Try camping in the desert and establish a connection. The land will carry you and provide you with information to go forward.

"You are far away from me, it is difficult to connect to you, I don't know more. Start to meditate and try to spend a few nights in the desert." Those were her words and then we hung up.

It was late summer, and the weather conditions were nice. I began searching the internet for any upcoming camping retreats and came across a retreat with a very dramatic name "Catharsis" led by a local shaman named Quynn Red Mountain.

Assessing my current situation, I signed up without any hesitation. It was ideal since I didn't want to be alone in open nature, and the retreat involved spending two nights south of Tucson on the reservation where Quynn had a small piece of land.

Before it all began, I established a simple morning routine to start my day. I realized that in times of uncertainty, engaging in repetitive, simple activities can provide a sense of stability. Every morning, I woke up and went for a swim at a local swimming pool, completing 10 laps, followed by the exact same breakfast. That helped me move forward. After breakfast, I started exploring my surroundings—cafes, restaurants, supermarkets, and parks. I needed to know what was around me to feel safer and more stable. With each passing day, things started to improve.

After more than a week, I discovered myself heading south to the retreat in open desert grasslands with the distant Baboquivari Peak, eagerly anticipating the experience.

—

Upon arrival, a group of seven, mostly women, gathered in the afternoon on the land. We collectively chose to disconnect from the digital world by turning off our phones, creating an atmosphere of intentional presence. Our gathering commenced with a shamanic drumming session in a dugout pit adorned with ornate fabrics. The setting resembled a scene from Persia, with one wall intentionally left exposed, showcasing the beautiful red earth embellished with stones and roots. Stepping into this space felt like descending into the depths of the earth itself. The dugout room offered a pleasantly cool ambiance, and we arranged ourselves on cushions as the rhythmic drumming began.

Bum,

Bum, Bum,

Bum, Bum, Bum,

Bum,

Bum, Bum,

Bum, Bum, Bum…

I laid down and covered myself with a light scarf. Here, it was much easier for me not to think. I entered a slightly hypnotic state.

In my mind, I saw a beautiful green forest full of ferns and found a tree with stairs leading to a lower ancient forest. It took me into a red underground corridor. Suddenly, I saw an image of my body lying on the red earth, from which roots were sprouting and penetrating the ground.

My body turned into a plant. At times, my hands felt like agave, then like mesquite tree leaves, and sometimes like blooming cactus flowers. I felt how the earth nourished me there, giving me trust and assurance, drawing life, moisture, and strength. I momentarily became a desert, completely merging with the sacred space around me.

I don't even know how long it took, but Quynn began to slow down and diminish the drumming, and gradually, we opened our eyes. It was time for sharing, but I couldn't even share. A heavy feeling overwhelmed me that I couldn't go back to yet. I needed to step away for a while and be alone. My process wasn't over. I expressed my intention to rejoin later and walked up the stairs to the ground, away from the group, my tears flowing.

I found a secluded spot and released that immense sadness. It was as if the earth were cleansing itself through me, and I through it. I witnessed dreadful scenes etched in my soul—violence, torn abdomens, blood, and screams. I gave it all to the earth, pleading for it to cleanse through my body and reclaim it. I was purging my past life and my fears—the brutal genocide that happened, the Indigenous one that is carried by my soul as distinct from my ancestral one.

My saliva and tears fell on the parched ground. I felt vulnerable, just like a piece of exposed meat. This was the most powerful experience of my journey. I was lying there, watching the sky until a profound sense of peace enveloped me. I finally understood why I came here—to reconcile with a previous death, and everything else was given to me as a reward.

Returning to the group, we continued with storytelling. Later, I found a secluded space for a natural shower, and Quynn, standing on a stone so that she was higher than me, slowly poured two buckets of water over me. That was the best shower of my life. Then, we played music and enjoyed the dark, starry night. I fell asleep to the sounds of didjeridoo and howling coyotes. It was one of the most beautiful nights I have experienced in the Sonoran desert.

The next day, we spent more time exploring nature and indulging in more music. It felt like a joyous reunion of a very old tribal gathering.

Pedaling On & Teeing Off: A Tucson Sporting Odyssey

with Kyle Trudeau, and Maya Benita

Upon my return, a sense of peace settled within me, yet the sensation lingered, akin to navigating chaos while teetering on a tightrope. Staying at home wasn't an option; I compelled myself to venture outside and explore. This decision led me to acquire a second-hand mountain bike, initiating a journey of discovering local trail systems. Nature became my solace, and with each passing day, I enthusiastically anticipated the surprises it held. Mountain biking brought me a lot of joy. While purchasing a helmet at a bike shop located in the foothills, I had the opportunity to meet Kyle, who worked there and helped me expand my biking world tremendously.

—

Kyle Trudeau, a Tucson local, developed a passion for bicycles at the age of three. His journey started with BMX racing at five, and soon transitioned to motocross racing until he took up racing bicycles full time at 21. Kyle has achieved success at the highest level of the sport in road cycling, mountain biking, and gravel racing. Notable highlights of his career include representing the USA at the World Championships of Marathon Mountain Bike in 2021, Single Speed Mountain Bike National Champion in 2015, and finishing 4th in the Whiskey Off-Road Pro Backcountry race.

—

Kyle was busy servicing a bike, so we decided to catch up at Le Buzz, a local hotspot, where bikers usually gather before they hit the road to Mt. Lemmon. We both biked there, and it was so fun to start learning cycling routes within town. Kyle was a biking enthusiast, and what intrigued me was his in-depth knowledge of various biking disciplines, including mountain biking, road biking, and gravel riding.

"What sets Tucson apart when it comes to biking?" I questioned.

He enthusiastically shared, "Tucson truly boasts a remarkably diverse landscape that lets you train on all sorts of terrain – mountain, pavement, gravel, steep, flat.… The conditions are perfect, especially in winter. That's why you get folks coming from out of town, even from Canada, for some training in this pleasant weather."

Nodding, I probed further, "And what about Mt. Lemmon? What's the deal with that?"

"Well," Kyle explained, "Picture a paved road stretching from the base to the summit, spanning approximately 30 miles of ascent. The journey takes you through diverse landscapes, from the arid desert below to the lush aspens and pines at the pinnacle. The allure of this route is immense. Additionally, the climate here becomes a game-changer, facilitating year-round training. While summers may bring the heat, early morning workouts remain feasible."

Curious, I asked, "So, what's the secret sauce of the Tucson cycling scene?"

"It's the community. Tucson's got a strong cycling community. It played a big role in my cycling journey. I grew up in motocross, lived in Tucson my whole life, but I didn't realize how awesome the cycling scene was until I dove in. It's something else."

"That's great! What are the best biking group rides or races?"

"The Shootout Group Road Bike Ride, a tradition spanning over thirty years, stands out as one of the largest and fastest group bike rides in the country. Departing every Saturday from downtown near the University of Arizona campus, it heads south down to Mission Road, extending into Green Valley before looping back around Sonoita and returning. This ride is like a mock race, and is a challenging event. While I can't say it's the only factor that makes

Tucson such an excellent training ground, it's certainly a major one because it is weekly.

"Another popular event is the 24 Hours in the Old Pueblo race for mountain biking, which has been running for two decades and attracts participants from around the world. Additionally, the Tucson Bicycle Classic is another long-standing race in the area. El Tour de Tucson is an incredible cycling race that serves as a showcase for what Tucson has to offer in terms of routes and community involvement."

"Where is the best place to experience the different terrains?"

"For road biking enthusiasts, Tucson offers a variety of routes that cater to different preferences. Venturing in any direction out of town or along the Tucson Loop Bicycle Path provides diverse options. Heading east allows you to tackle the challenging ascent of Mt. Lemmon, while the southern route takes you towards Green Valley and Sahuarita. Here, you'll discover low-traffic roads that are both flat and well-maintained. If you prefer a western journey, crossing Gates Pass opens up exploration of the Tucson Mountains—an option less daunting than the towering Mt. Lemmon.

"When it comes to gravel biking," he continued, "there's close proximity to Patagonia, which has gained popularity in the gravel biking scene. Here, you'll discover endless miles of lightly traveled gravel roads, offering a perfect escape from in-town traffic and hustle.

"And for mountain bikers, the diversity is astonishing. You can find a trail just 15 minutes from downtown. Heading west, explore the Sweetwater trail system with flowing and slightly rocky trails. The Tucson Mountains offer rugged rocky terrain, especially around Starr Pass." Kyle enthusiastically pointed out these areas on the map and continued, "If you prefer smoother trails, there's Fantasy Island in the east, and the HoneyBee trail system far to the north. One of my favorites is the 50-Year trail up north, offering a diverse experience with good flow, technical sections, and unique features like big boulder rock rolls, exclusive to this area. If you're up for a technical challenge, Mt. Lemmon has a wide variety of trails to push your technical skills."

"Who are some of the famous bikers who train in Tucson?"

"During the winter, Tucson becomes a magnet for cycling enthusiasts from all over the country, including some well-known names in the cycling world. Among those who spend their winters here are Keegan Swenson, Russell Finsterwald, and Howard Grotts, all of whom are prominent figures in the off-road cycling community. Additionally, Tucson is a favored training destination for accomplished triathlon athletes like Ben Hoffman, Sam Long, and many others."

"What's important for mountain biking here? How should I be equipped?"

"When you're out riding, having a solid, full suspension bike with tubeless tires is a game changer, especially with all those sharp rocks on the trails. Consider going for some heavy-duty tires to handle the rugged terrain. And don't forget your water bottle. Most trails don't have water stops, so you've got to bring your hydration game."

"These are great tips!" We finished our coffee, said our goodbyes, and I thanked Kyle for the insightful advices.

—

Biking turned out to be an excellent choice for me. Taking Kyle's advice, I switched to puncture-proof tires, eliminating worries about pesky glass or prickly cacti ruining my ride.

I connected with various biking groups and explored diverse routes like The Loop, Sweetwater Preserve, Honey Bee, Fantasy Land, and 50-Year Trail. Joining the Tuesday evening bike rides, starting at the flagpole at the U of A fountain, became a regular source of joy, leading to the formation of new friendships.

Biking through many neighborhoods in town revealed different facets of Tucson that I had not known before; some neighborhoods were affluent, while others were notably impoverished and unkempt.

The experience added a layer of depth to my understanding of the city's diversity, and I began to grasp why fate guided me through this change. Living in the beautiful foothills, I could never fully comprehend the town's essence.

However, my favorite biking experiences were the night rides in the desert. Those nights when it's just you and a few friends, the starry sky, the howling coyotes, passing tarantulas, and the outlines of huge cacti. Those were some of the best and most adventurous nights I had. There's not a day or night wasted when spent on the saddle of a bicycle. Mountain biking, in particular, became a grounding force, helping me navigate through all the changes and uncertainties.

My newfound outgoing nature and the friendships formed through biking led me to campus, where, in a coffee shop, I had the pleasure of meeting Maya through a common friend. Our conversation was fueled by shared knowledge and a personal connection to the Skyline Country Club. It brought back fond memories of sitting on a terrace, enjoying the sounds of teeing off, or spending time with friends at a putting range next to the Clubhouse. This unexpected connection wove another thread into the fabric of my Tucson experience.

—

Maya Benita, a Tucson native, found her love for golf at the age of 14 following a soccer injury. Her high-level competitive journey in gold took off with a significant victory at the AZ Division II State Championship during her senior year at Catalina Foothills HS, setting a record for the lowest score in Tucson girls' state championship history. Notably, Maya is one of three female golfers from Tucson competing at the NCAA Division 1 level. She is pursuing a Finance degree from the Eller College of Business at the University of Arizona and is a 3X WGCA Scholar All-American. Additionally, she currently serves as the voice of student-athletes on the University of AZ Executive Board of the Student-Athlete Advisory Committee. As the Chair of Community Service, she provides input on institutional, conference and national issues.

—

Maya and I planned to meet at the University of Arizona campus to stroll around the park. Wandering amid the iconic red-brick buildings, Maya guided me through vibrant campus culture. The air buzzing with the pride of fellow students dressed up in their Arizona Wildcats gear, immersing us in the heartbeat of university life.

Delightful weather complemented the picturesque setting of gnarled olive and carob trees and palm-lined streets of the original old campus.

"What sets Tucson's golf experience apart from other destinations?" I asked curiously as we were strolling the campus.

"I would say the kind of golf we play here—it is desert golf. There are only a few places in the world where you can play this kind of golf, which is equally beautiful and punishing. If you are not hitting shots to the right parts of a golf course, you are dealing with cactus, sand, all sorts of animals, and of course sometimes, enormous heat. It is a very precise kind of golf, but it is also beautiful. It is fascinating how every course has its own unique desert-style layout.

"Tucson golf is also special because of the community. Golf has a large presence across town, and pretty much everyone has at least tried playing golf, knows a golfer or has played in a tournament. Whenever you say you are on the golf team at U of A, there is a tight community of people who have your back, who are always supporting you, and cheering you on as we play around the world."

"How would you describe your style? What techniques do you use to stay focused?"

"I loved watching Lexi Thompson growing up because of how strong she was. She is a very powerful golfer, and that is how I would describe myself. I may not always be the most accurate, but I am strong and powerful. I am great off the tee, and known for having a very good short game. So even if I am not the most accurate, I can usually get up and down and hit shots close to the hole from anywhere around the green.

"Honestly, golf is a very frustrating sport. You get easy shots and you get hard shots. You really can't control where the ball ends up. It is like with life—you can't control what happens, only how you react to it. I would say I like playing in the desert because when I do get frustrated or have a tough day, it is so easy to look up at the mountains and saguaros and just remember where I am.

"Staying present and appreciative is my strongest technique. When I look up and see the incredible Catalina Mountains, it is just so hard to be mad at this game. You cannot be thinking about a few holes ahead or a few holes behind. You just have to focus on what you are doing at the moment."

"Indeed, clever ways of responding to life's curveballs," I thought. "Are there specific golf courses or holes in Tucson that you find particularly enjoyable?"

"I grew up playing at La Paloma and Skyline Country Club, which are both up in the Catalina Foothills. Each course offers unique features, hole designs, views, and types of tees. La Paloma CC is a Jack Nicklaus designed golf course. I think one of the prettiest holes I have ever been on is number seven on the Hill Course. It is a challenging, risk-reward Par 5, and it has the best view in the city. Other than that, Ventana Canyon CC is probably the most unique golf course and has one of the coolest holes. There is a 100-yard-long Par 3 that's carved right into the mountains.

"A lesser-known gem would be a golf course called The Gallery, which is way up north. It is private, so it is hard to get a tee time— but a must play if the opportunity arises."

"So…what advice or tips would you give to newcomers?"

"My advice is to embrace the uniqueness of Tucson's golf style with patience. It is unlike anything else in the country, and there will be a learning curve, particularly when playing in the firm and fast desert conditions for the first few times. Be ready for some new golf shots, and most importantly, have fun.

"Remember, it's not just about how well you play, but the breathtaking views and the distinctiveness of Tucson golf that you can enjoy. If your ball comes to rest in a desert 'rough', I would say just get out as quickly as possible and don't try to take on more than you can. As my dad always says, 'Take your medicine.' Whenever you encounter challenges in the desert, take the most direct path out. Be cautious of the cacti, thorns, blooming plants, and the presence of rattlesnakes in the summer."

"An important heads-up," I mused appreciatively. We walked towards the U of A main flagpole and decided to sit by the beautiful fountain.

"What has been your experience studying for the U of A and being an athlete? Do you have time to watch other sports?"

"Balancing academics and 20 hours of golf practice per week is definitely challenging. It's like having a full-time job; you have to love it, and I do. I have a deep appreciation for the school and its historic program. Our team is incredibly diverse, with girls from 7 different countries. Being in such an environment is not only inspiring but also a learning experience about various cultures and, most importantly, about myself.

"We've all become close friends, and our daily breakfasts in the athlete cafeteria have played a big part in that. Fortunately, we have a strong athletics program, and I enjoy watching and supporting other sports. I'm a big sports fan. I like basketball, football, and volleyball, and try to go to as many of those games as possible. But it is golf that gives me the greatest love of the desert."

Meeting Maya was a truly transformative experience, especially during my transitional times. Her presence was powerful, exuding confidence and focus.

Eager to explore more social aspects of Tucson, I asked her about parties and festivals. She enthusiastically recommended Tucson Meet Yourself, which was conveniently scheduled for the upcoming weekend. The prospect of immersing myself in a festival celebrating

Tucson's diverse cultural heritage added an exciting dimension to my journey, and I looked forward to experiencing the atmosphere and engaging with the local community.

—

When I headed downtown for this big event, I was pleasantly surprised by its sheer size and the multitude of people in attendance. The central streets of Tucson underwent a magical transformation into a lively street gathering, brimming with an array of food and music. Taking my time, I strolled around, exploring the various stands, and decided to indulge in some Asian dumplings and a refreshing drink. Eventually, I found a spot at one of the stages where captivating performances unfolded, including African drumming and violin. Later, a particularly intriguing performance was starting, showcasing the deer dance from the Yaqui tribe.

As I sat engrossed in the cultural displays, an older man in the front row on a mobility scooter addressed the audience through a microphone, sternly announcing that photography and video recording were not allowed at that moment. He also provided a very personal and insightful introduction to the Yaqui culture.

After the breathtaking show, my curiosity was piqued. I couldn't resist approaching the big man on the mobility scooter as he had introduced the Yaqui dancers with such heart. I wanted to understand more about the restrictions and to learn about the cultural significance behind the performances. This is how I had the pleasure of meeting Big Jim Griffith.

Spices of Identity: Folkloric Threads, Savory Enchiladas & Melting-Pot Narratives

with James Griffith, Michael Hultquist Jr., and Martha Ames Burgess

—

James Griffith, known to his many friends as Big Jim, earned three degrees at the University of Arizona, including a PhD in Cultural Anthropology and Art History. He was an author, academic, public folklorist, and member of multiple Tucson cultural organizations. He served as a Director of the Southwest Folklore Center and founded the annual Tucson Meet Yourself Festival. For nearly five decades, he devoted himself to the study and honor of the Sonoran people's folklore, work that earned him the Bess Lomax Hawes Prize for "significant contribution to the preservation and awareness of cultural heritage." His nine published books include the titles Hecho a Mano, Saints of the Southwest, and Saints, Statues and Stories.

—

Jim was occupied with festival activities, and we decided that I would visit their house a week after the dust cleared. He gave me Loma's, his wife's, number. Later, I called her, and we set up a meeting at their home near San Xavier del Bac Mission.

As the appointed day arrived, I discovered myself driving south toward this scenic mission, also known as "The White Dove of the Desert". The journey took me past an ancient graveyard and through the captivating desert landscape. The trip itself became an enriching experience, and meeting Jim and his wife, Loma, at their home proved to be even more extraordinary.

97

Jim was sitting under the ramada, while Loma made us some tea. A dog came to greet us, and during our interview there was the constant sound of chirping birds, which were playing among the surrounding sheltering mesquite trees.

"Oh, you're from Czechoslovakia! So you're probably familiar with a band in Tucson called the Bouncing Czechs!"

"Haha!" I laughed at the clever name. "No, I have missed them!"

"That's a Czech-Slovac band formed in Tucson, playing European Polkas and Waltzes."

"I bet they are great. I hope to see them performing next time!"

Jim paused looked into my eyes directly and quietly said out of the blue, "So, do you want to hear a story about Father Garcés and his picture?"

"Oh, yes. I am ready to listen," I replied, settling into a comfortable chair and sipping my tea.

"So, Anza made this big march from Tucson to San Francisco Bay, essentially testing out the overland trail to California. He led a full military company, accompanied by various individuals, including Father Garcés, a Franciscan missionary priest. Father Garcés was fervently dedicated to introducing the new religion to the people along the way. To aid in his mission, he had a special painting created, depicting the Blessed Virgin Mary offering help on one side and illustrating Purgatory on the other. He used this painting as a tool for preaching."

Jim paused for a bit. "And that picture is in Tucson."

"That's incredible. And how did it happened?"

"Because when he came back to Tucson, he went to Yuma, stationed as a missionary, and that's where he was also murdered."

"Why was he murdered?" I interrupted.

"He was killed by Native Americans because his predecessor did not follow through with a promised deal, and they revolted. So, they killed him, although he was a peace maker. But before he was killed, he gave his beautiful picture to his godson, who was the commandant of the Tucson Presidio, and it stayed within the same family.

"That's what this community is like. So much is here, very quietly, but this is what we have here. This is a part of Tucson's folklore."

"That's an amazing story… So, what does folklore actually mean?"

Jim spoke very slowly and with interest: "The term folklore covers the informal side of human creativity, the culture that groups—even relatively small groups—create for their own purposes and which reflects the group's traditional values and beliefs. If you are inside the culture, it is the everyday stuff you are familiar with; if you are outside the culture it can seem exotic and fascinating.

"Folklore includes language, beliefs, stories, dances, jokes, games and much more. For example, family folklore could be code words with special meanings within the family or the stories about family members, living and dead, that get told and retold. While this knowledge is maintained and passed along over time, it is not static but dynamic, constantly changing in response to the present environment. Because the folklore of a place reflects the people who live there, every place has its own unique folklore."

"Why is it so important to preserve and respect cultures and traditions?"

"There is a saying: it is easier to walk a road if there is a surface under your feet. Culture and tradition give us stability, connection, emphasizing the importance of family and the extended community. Perhaps the only thing more important than knowing one's roots is mutual respect.

"Respect enables us to go beyond and meet each other at the crossroads. Openness to seeing others' ways of doing things has long been a Tucson tradition. Decades ago, while emceeing at a small shopping mall concert, I introduced a popular Native American

Tohono O'odham (then called Papago[3]) band. Daniel Joaquin took over the microphone and announced, 'We are the Joaquin Brothers, Papago Indians from way out west on the Reservation, and we try to play lively music. We hope you will make us welcome, because, after all, we made you welcome!'

"And over the centuries this openness has opened doors to deeper mutual understanding. Culture is coded, and different cultures have different codes. Living among diverse local groups, I have delighted in attending the performance of a bilingual, bicultural merchant shifting between Hispanic and Anglo customers, as I watched him pivot not only his spoken language, but his entire body language from initial greetings through sales presentation to farewell embrace or handshake.

"By living for years next to members of the Yaqui tribe of Native Americans I have come to appreciate that while in Western cultures crossed arms mean 'closed off' or 'unreceptive', by contrast Yaqui elders with crossed arms are a sign of respect, 'I am listening to you, this is an important conversation.' I initially chose Tucson as my home because I was intrigued by its exciting cultural diversity, and my life has been immeasurably enriched by these insights."

"Why is Tucson Meet Yourself so successful—so unique?"

"The festival is unique because Tucson is unique. Here we share the excitement we feel as we experience our region's diversity. We are trying to do one thing, and that is to spread respect and understanding of the living traditional cultures and their aesthetic expressions here in Southern Arizona. It is a celebration of the richness and diversity of the living traditions and arts of local ethnic and folk communities, such as African-Americans, Tohono O'odham, Yaqui, cowboys, bikers, and other groups which share some commonality like a system of communication, arts, and, of course, food. For the past four decades, the three-day festival has

---

[3] The term "Papago" has its origins in Spanish and was historically used to mean "the bean eaters." It is an external name imposed on the Tohono O'odham people by Spanish colonizers.

transformed a few downtown streets into a celebration of regional folklife with food vendors, visual artists, craftspeople, dancers, singers, and exhibitors, recently hosting more than 100,000 visitors to experience these cultural crossroads and that is what I love about it the most."

"What would you say is the essence of Tucson? What are its signature features?"

"Like any other city, Tucson is a complicated place. It has strong Indigenous foundations, and a rich infusion of Mediterranean influences. Not to forget its abundant cultural ties that binds it all to the places modern Tucsonans originally came from. Our local language is peppered with words like mesquite, saguaro and rodeo, and our billboards show Yaqui deer dancer images and the Tohono O'odham labyrinth. Go to a Mexican restaurant and you'll be very hard pressed to find a standard dish that doesn't involve the colors of the Mexican flag. The red enchiladas will be topped with chopped green onions and white sour cream, and may even be called '*enchiladas estilo bandera*' (flag-style enchiladas). These details point to the strong cohesive ties to Indigenous or Mexican."

"Where do *you* think is the best place to taste Mexican food?"

"Go to South Tucson; there are plenty of family-owned Mexican restaurants," Jim suggested.

It was only later that I realized I had been given a special gift, to meet one of Tucson's legends, and I was deeply moved to hear that he had passed some time after our interview.

We exchanged our goodbyes, and the warmth of our meeting lingered as I continued driving through Tucson. The thought of Big Jim's enchiladas "*estilo bandera*" stayed with me, prompting me to make another stop and explore one of the Mexican restaurants in South Tucson. A quick Google search led me to El Torero, where I had the pleasure to meet Michael Hultquist Jr.

Michael Hultquist Jr., also known as Mikey, is a co-owner of El Torero restaurant, and the previous co-owner of Lerua's Mexican restaurant which was serving Tucson traditional Mexican food for almost 100 years. In 2015, Michael Jr. earned a degree from San Diego School of Culinary Arts, an intensive six-month program that favors technique over recipes, and mandates studying all aspects of running a successful restaurant.

—

When I arrived at El Torero, both Michael Jr. and Michael Sr. were on-site, actively involved in the family business and dedicated to the art of cooking. The atmosphere exuded a genuine family vibe, transporting me to the heart of Mexico. The authenticity of the setting, combined with the savory aroma of traditional Mexican dishes, created a special dining experience. As I relished the *sabores*, Mikey, sensing my enjoyment, expressed interest in my thoughts on the food. Seizing the opportunity, I didn't hesitate to reciprocate the curiosity.

Curious to unravel the narrative behind the delicious dishes and the familial warmth that characterized El Torero, I inquired, "What is the story of your family restaurant?"

"We used to have three restaurants. Only this one, El Torero, is still operating. Lerua's was here for almost 100 years, and its history is somewhat intertwined with our family members running it, including our aunts and uncles. It used to be an institution for some people, a tried-and-true place, as we had our ups and downs, but the food was consistently good. The recipes have stayed the same over time."

"In all of your history, what are you most proud of?"

"Our greatest achievement is the ability to continue the legacy. El Torero is one of the oldest restaurants in South Tucson. Its history is connected to my grandmother, who, feeling somewhat bored at home, decided to purchase a restaurant. After working at Lerua's for 40 years to prove to her husband that she could do it, she ended up buying Lerua's, and subsequently, she opened El Torero. That's how we truly got into the business."

"What do you think forms the core of traditional Mexican cuisine?"

"The core of Mexican cuisine lies in the skill and technique used to cook the dishes. It doesn't really matter what you're cooking; it depends on specific recipes and, of course, the right ingredients. The location also plays a crucial role. It's about the region of Mexico and the recipes specific to those areas, as well as the ingredients grown there.

"*Mole* sauce can be considered a 'mother sauce' in Mexican cuisine, similar to *béchamel* in French cuisine. *Mole* is a complex mixture of spices and ingredients, creating a rich and flavorful sauce. In certain parts of Mexico, *moles* are made from blends of chilies, specific spices, nuts, and sometimes chocolate. These ingredients are boiled, blended, and served.

"In other provinces, the same ingredients are boiled, roasted, and served. Sometimes, they are puréed and then thickened to create different variations. The diversity of Mexican cuisine comes from the customs of each province. If you are in Sinaloa or Sonora, you'll find varying recipes because they use what is readily available in their regions. The resulting taste is derived from the unique recipes, cooking techniques, and locally-sourced ingredients. For example, Sonora has excellent cattle, so *carne asada* is a popular dish there. But if you visit Oaxaca, you won't find beef on the menu; instead, you'll enjoy delicious seafood dishes."

"What is the difference between Mexican food in Mexico and Mexican food in Tucson?"

"When you come to Tucson, our take on those dishes will be very different because we have access to special borderlands ingredients that allow us to experiment. Traditionalism can be challenging with food because recipes often involve copying someone else, but it's the tweaks and adjustments that truly make a dish unique. Mexican cuisine offers an array of ingredients, and how you use them and the techniques you apply create a new and innovative take on the dishes.

"Mexico's culinary repertoire includes a wide variety of ingredients such as chili, tomatoes, and different types of squashes, dried chilies, grains, and beans. The tortilla is to Mexico what a *baguette* is to France. Each region uses proteins, spices, and unique techniques to craft their signature dishes. The essence lies in learning these techniques from different areas and then incorporating them into our own culinary creations.

"Tucson boasts many family-owned restaurants, where the owners proudly showcase their cultural roots. This fusion of traditions is what makes our culinary scene so wonderful. We use ingredients, like real farmers' cheese or homemade sour cream. With such a mix and match of regional Mexican influences, Tucson boasts on its road signs 'the best 23 miles of Mexican food in the U.S.'"

"What are some of your local heritage dishes?"

"Some of the oldest dishes 'native' to Tucson would undoubtedly be *nana tacos*, which are deep-fried ground beef in hard shells. It's an ancient way of cooking. Back then, someone filled toasted tortillas with meat and mashed potatoes. We're talking about food that started off in very humble surroundings, almost what people would consider peasant foods. They were very inexpensive to make because they needed to feed a lot of people. Here, you'll find dishes like *flautas* (taquitos), *patty tacos, sopas, cheese crisps*, and *flat enchiladas*. These are delicacies that the older class grew up eating. Another iconic dish is *tamales*, starchy and usually corn-based *masa* or dough, steamed in a corn husk. The staple here is definitely green corn.

"Fresh corn masa tamales are quite challenging to make, a challenge we embrace, and that's one of the reasons Lerua's stood the test of time. The key lies in the process of grinding the corn. While some opt for blending, the majority, including us, use the traditional stone mill. Crafting tamales takes 11 hours, yet they are savored in just 5 minutes. The 'Sonoran style' we offer is characterized by its simplicity, drawing nuances from various regions but presented here with minimal ingredients."

"How would you describe Mexican culture here in Tucson? And what holidays do you celebrate?"

"A significant aspect of Tucson is its primarily Hispanic population. The city's hot and spread-out nature leads to many cultural activities taking place inside households. While Sunday masses and weddings are held in churches, and family gatherings occur in parks, most cultural events happen in homes, where good food plays a central role. The celebration of the Day of the Dead (*Día de Muertos*) differs significantly between Mexico and the U.S. In Tucson, which is a big one- or two-day festival, whereas in Mexico, it spans over two weeks.

"During the Tucson Día de Muertos celebration, we set up shrines, light candles, and ensure our ancestors are acknowledged and remembered. It's a meaningful celebration for them.

"When visiting Mexico, the focus of celebrations is on our ancestors as well, but we also explore the food, scenery, beaches, museums, cathedrals, and Aztec ruins. Several significant Hispanic celebrations in Tucson include Semana Santa (Easter Week), Las Posadas (A Christmas tradition involving processions), New Year's, the Festival of Xilonen (following the Aztec calendar), Padre Kino Celebration, Cinco de Mayo, and Mexican Independence Day (Día de la Independencia). These events hold great importance in honoring our traditions and history."

"Where do *you* go to eat in town for Mexican food?"

"When it comes to Mexican food, if I'm not cooking it myself, I enjoy dining at Mariscos Chihuahua, Tacos Apson, and The Little One. However, since I often cook Mexican dishes at home, I like to explore Korean cuisine, and Kimchi Time is one of my favorites. Another favorite spot is Maynards Market by the railroad, where I can sit on the patio and enjoy the ambiance. Five Points Market and Restaurant is also fantastic for its unique fusions. Despite all these choices, my absolute favorite place to eat is in my own kitchen. I simply love cooking."

As Mikey excused himself to return to the kitchen, he began preparing dishes for a group of newly arrived patrons.

Driving home, a cloud of anxiety about my move still hung over my thoughts. With only three weeks until I had to vacate, the reality of time constraints weighed on me, creating a sense of urgency. Uncertain about the exact duration I would need, I decided to seek help from friends.

Fortunately, Lisa, one of my friends, came to the rescue. She presented a thoughtful solution: I could stay at the home of our mutual friend Martha, affectionately known as Muffin. Since Muffin had plans for an extended trip, I could take care of her garden during her absence.

This arrangement not only provided me with a practical place to stay but also promised a unique experience on the far West Side of Tucson. It felt like a reassuring solution to the uncertainties I was facing, turning out to be a more enjoyable and interesting choice than a hotel.

—

Martha Ames Burgess, also known as Muffin, is an ethnobotanist, ecologist, artist, and a great cook. She has a BA from Brown University in geosciences and a masters from the University of Arizona in the field of dendrochronology. Mentored by Tohono O'odham Elders, Martha came into ethnobotany from the inside out, learning how to harvest, prepare, store, and eat many Sonoran Desert edibles. With Tohono O'odham farmers and Native Seeds/SEARCH cofounders, she was taught desert gardening with native heirlooms. She has shared her ethnobotanical knowledge as an adjunct at Tohono O'odham Community College, and through native-foods workshops for Tucson's Mission Garden.

—

Before Muffin left for her trip, she treated me to a delightful dinner featuring heirloom O'odham pink bean tostadas with Cholla Buds infused with a Cajun flair. I had never tasted better beans.

As we sat on her terrace, I took advantage of the relaxed setting to ask her questions and soak in the comforting atmosphere of her home. Given Muffin's expertise as an ethnobotanist and a cook, I seized the opportunity to dive deeper and asked her about local cuisine and crops.

"Muffin, how would you describe local cuisine?"

"Aaaah" Muffin smiled warmly, "Well, that's not an easy one," she paused for a while, and then began to explain:

"There are so many different facets to Tucson's local cuisine: southwestern 'nouvelle', Mexican with deep Hispanic roots, and traditional Native American, specifically O'odham, plus Chinese, African. We are building on ten thousand years of tradition here! Over the last 5000 years or so until the European invasion, the food focus began to shift from wild hunted-gathered foods to incorporate cultivated crops into the Native diet—crops domesticated here by Native People of the New World!

"With colonization in the 17th Century, Spanish missionaries had a significant influence adding their imported foods to an already complex regional diet, followed by Sonoran-Mexican, European, African, and Anglo-American with the Gadsden Purchase, and Chinese with the railroad."

I listened intently, captivated by the layers of history and culture embedded in Tucson's local cuisine that were being revealed. Muffin's insights painted a vivid picture of the diverse flavors and influences that had shaped the region's culinary identity over the centuries.

She continued, "With these waves of culture, Tucson's cuisine has grown incredibly rich and multi-layered, offering a wide array of flavors. Our food palette features sustained-energy starches, tantalizing spiciness that excites the taste buds, substantial vegetable

107

proteins, and natural complex sweetness. Tucson is truly a melting pot of diverse culinary traditions! I envision it as this colorful 'taste-macramé' with all these strands weaving and knotting themselves into interesting new culinary patterns and combinations."

"What are some of the traditional heritage crops and how are they processed?"

"Cacti have been a part of the Sonoran Desert environment for at least 8000-9000 years, and significant to Native cuisine. Succulent young pads (stems) of prickly pear cacti are highly nutritious and are typically cooked as *nopalitos*, while the fruits are processed into sweet syrup or dried as fruit-leather. The giant saguaro cactus provides more than energizing fruit—the saguaro harvest is a spiritual time when the Indigenous O'odham come together to share a sacred brew from the fruit and pray for rain.

"Tucson is probably one of the few places you may get served Cholla Cactus Buds. The short spring season of cholla flowering provides spiny buds that have to be very carefully gathered, despined and arduously prepared, resulting in a super-food staple, known to Desert People forever, and now being rediscovered by culinary artists for pickles, *quiches, hors d'oeuvres.*

"Traditionally, the O'odham cultivated summer crops including corn, beans, and squash in their water-harvested monsoon gardens. These 'three sisters' form the foundation of local cuisines well beyond Indigenous Nation boundaries. The sweetness and starchiness of corn were central to many dishes, the core ingredient for flatbreads and for porridge called *atole*. Squash also offers added vitamins along with delightful sweetness and starches.

"Heirloom beans bring a rich and diverse range of flavors, each variety showcasing its own unique character. Some beans have smokiness, some sweetness, others have a hardiness with protein richness. They come in different shapes, colors, patterns, and sizes, offering a diversity of possible dishes."

"What about the legume trees?"

"Legume trees are a hallmark of the Southwest desert, producing pods rich in nutrition. Mesquite trees, for example, yield dry pods that can be milled into gluten-free flour. The desert soil also brings forth a wild plant called *chiltepin*, which is the genetic precursor of most domestic chili peppers. Over the years, people have selected divergent varieties, resulting in a wide range of savory excitement. The tiny *chiltepin* pepper, harvested carefully from unassuming wild bushes, gives a quick blast of flavor along with a wild but short-lived kick!"

"What happened next when the other cultures arrived?"

"When colonial Europeans invaded what is now southern Arizona Borderlands, they introduced grains such as wheat, which certainly became an important part of the diet. It was adopted early on because it provided food during a formerly lean time of year. Sonorans and Tucsonans were able to grow it in their winter gardens and embraced it as a new staple, with their favorite use being a wheat-flour tortilla. Father Kino and later missionaries brought a diversity of Old World food-plants for hopeful experimentation in this new mission territory—seeds from Africa and various parts of the Mediterranean.

"The Sonoran Desert experiences winter rains as well. However, before the contact period, the O'odham did not cultivate winter crops. Missionaries introduced winter active English peas, lentils, chards, barley. They introduced fruit trees like quince, pomegranate, figs, and dates, along with long-season melons, which were warmly welcomed by the O'odham. These foreign vegetables and fruits became essential, filling a void in both agriculture and nutrition. Spanish cuisine played a vital role in completing the agricultural calendar.

"Concurrently, the military arrived, establishing forts like El Presidio de Tucson and bringing livestock such as sheep and cattle to complement existing Native protein sources. Anglos, African-Americans, and cowboys arrived later, introducing camp foods like

109

bacon, biscuits, and coffee that could withstand the chuckwagon lifestyle and move with the cows.

"The arrival of the railroad in 1880 brought Chinese influence, particularly notable in Tucson due to truck gardens, also known as market gardens. These were small-scale vegetable or fruit farms that typically grew produce for direct sale to consumers. In the 1930s-40s, my O'odham mentor recalled Chinese truck gardeners supplying fresh vegetables to both the reservation and Tucson, contributing to the availability of fresh veggies.

"Each new 'culture-wave' into the Tucson area through our history has brought a set of delicious new food items to cultivate and add to Tucson's culinary palette!"

"Fascinating! What are the most typical Tucson dishes?"

"The first item you'll find on the menu isn't *haute cuisine*; it's a burrito!

"Burritos, which can be filled with almost anything, typically include beans with beef or pork, along with other ingredients like lettuce, sour cream, cheese, and guacamole, all wrapped in a flour tortilla.

"Another Tucson specialty is the *chimichanga*, a variation of a burrito that involves folding a flour tortilla in a way that allows it to be deep-fried. There are various stories about its origins, with one prevailing theory suggesting that Carlotta Flores' aunt, the former owner of El Charro Café, accidentally dropped a burrito into the fryer and exclaimed: 'chimichanga!' instead of 'Chinga tu madre!,' mindful of the presence of kids. However, the origin of 'chimichanga' remains a hot topic argument in Southwestern gastronomy. Everybody has a story. Regardless, it's undeniably super-delicious!

"*Quesadillas* are big here, consisting of a tortilla covered with cheese and toasted. Then there'll be tacos, filled with *carnitas* (long-roasted pork or beef), or *carne asada* (grilled beef), wrapped with toppings in a crispy corn tortilla. You can also get chicken or shrimp tacos. Always on top of these dishes you'll have other interesting deckings like strips of green chiles or avocado and cheese. Combinations are endless. I must also mention two little must-have side dishes: *Frijoles* (cooked, mashed beans), and *calabacitas* (chunked up, steamed and fried squash with melted cheese, sometimes with tomatoes, corn and onions). Both are wonderful.

"Of course, there's the Sonoran hotdog, dressed with chili beans, onions, and *salsa picante*. As for fancier things, yes, definitely, the prickly pear margarita! Now there are even people who are making prickly pear margarita salts, for the rim of your margarita glass. And if you want to get really local with your margarita, you can use *Bacanora* instead of tequila, which is a mezcal made from nearby roasted, fermented, distilled *wild agave*."

"And for desserts?"

"*Flan* is essentially like *crème brûlée*, our caramelized sweet-cream dessert. *Empanadas* (fruit or sweetened pumpkin turnovers) are another local favorite."

"Where would *you* go to eat?"

"The Mosaic Cafe and its spinoff Mosaic Cafe Dos are family Mexican restaurants with lots of Sonoran dishes, steeped in Tucson tradition. Hotel Congress' Cup Cafe is also a go-to for local creative fare—amazing sides of Barrio Bread's award-winning sourdoughs, made with local organic heirloom flours. The Arizona Inn is a special place, started in 1930s, with fine traditional and innovative dishes. Several Tucson resorts and country clubs have wonderful dining with a local, traditional flair, such as Hacienda del Sol.

"I also like Café à La C'Art next to Tucson Museum of Art for its historic location as well as sense-of-place dishes. Pat's Chili Dogs in Menlo Neighborhood provides local color. El Torero, Mi Nidito, Crossroads, Little Mexico—lots of home-style Sonoran-Mexican restaurants on Tucson's south and southwest sides—are great venues for local food, drink and atmosphere."

As darkness settled, Muffin handed me her keys and provided a brief tour of her home, pointing out essential details to make my stay comfortable. Knowing that I would be settling in a week brought a profound sense of relief, alleviating the uncertainties that had loomed over me.

Reward

Moving into Muffin's house was a truly delightful experience. The fired-adobe structure with wooden decorative columns exuded a unique charm. Its authenticity was accentuated by the spacious landscape of full grown saguaros, agaves, barrel cacti and mesquite trees that added to its overall appeal. Passing through the gate, a hitching post adorned with hanging chile peppers extended a warm welcome, immediately establishing the cozy and inviting atmosphere.

Unpacking my belongings, it felt like settling into a vacation at a granny's house, where each corner held a story and a touch of nostalgia. As I explored the rooms, a pleasant surprise awaited me in the form of a fridge and pantry stocked with every kind of exotic-looking food, potion or remedy crafted from various desert herbs.

On the pantry shelf, alongside jars of pickled cholla buds, there were homegrown garlic cucumbers, chiltepin-infused chocolate, and syrups made from wild dates. In the fridge beside mesquite-membrillo marmalade, there were hydrosols of desert lavender and Hopi mint-sage, creosote bush tinctures and infused jojoba oils. The thing is, it wasn't "exotic" at all—only to me. This was "local color", as local as it gets!

A handwritten note: "Feel free to taste anything that looks enticing to you," was on the table with a few other notes and instructions. It was such a reward.

Another treasure revealed itself in the meticulously organized library, categorized by genre. From volumes on Sonoran desert plants to Southwestern cuisine, Native American culture, cowboys, birding, and desert reptiles, each book hinted at the Sonoran Desert.

Through the library, I discovered the works of culinary artist Carolyn Niethammer, author-philosopher Gary Paul Nabhan, vocal environmentalist Edward Abbey, water harvester Brad Lancaster, herbalist Michael Moore, desert writer Joseph Wood Krutch, and many more. The walls were decorated with art depicting local Native Americans, including Tohono O'odham baskets, Yaqui masks, Hopi Kachinas, including many artworks created by Muffin and her mother, also a watercolor artist. This visual tapestry was so inspiring, and all of it felt like it was designed for my journey.

One day, when a storm hit, bringing its sudden change in humidity, a delightful scent wafted through the air, emanating from the *creosote bush*. Fascinated by this natural "perfume" so typical of the desert, I stepped outside to smell it and was met with a stunning view of Tucson delicately spread across the valley below.

Deciding to explore further, I walked westward, where the mountains arose nearby, and the sunset unfolded into a breathtaking spectacle. It was during this magical moment that I was at Muffin's house—a vantage point where the sun bids its daily farewell.

Rhythmic Rituals: Yaqui Culture & the Deer Dance

with Brandon Valera, and Raymond Buelna

As I delved into the intricacies of the Yaqui masks, a strong desire to deepen my understanding of Yaqui culture took hold. I realized that my encounter during the Tucson Meet Yourself festival had only piqued my interest. Hungry for more knowledge, I embarked on a quest to discover a museum exclusively devoted to Yaqui heritage. This pursuit led me to the Old Pascua Museum, where I had the pleasure of meeting Brandon.

—

Brandon Valera is the Director and Head Curator of the Old Pascua Museum Yaqui Culture Center, located in the historic Pascua Village in midtown Tucson. He graduated from the Institute for American Indian Arts, Santa Fe, in 2018 with a Bachelors of Fine Arts. His great-grandfather, Frank Ochoa, was one of the tribal leaders as well as a ceremonial captain in the Old Pascua Yaqui cultural society. Old Pascua Village has just been recognized in 2021 by the United States government as a federal tribal land. Brandon has been a part of the museum since 2019 and has helped with the preservation and education of Yaqui history and culture.

—

A few days later, I hopped into the car and drove to the Old Pascua Museum. It was a quaint adobe structure in the heart of Tucson, appearing seemingly deserted. However, as I opened the door, a young man named Brandon was sitting inside.

"Hi, my name is Brandon," he greeted me warmly and invited me into the museum. When I expressed my interest in Yaqui art, he began showcasing various artifacts, including pictures of a deer dancer, rattles, violins, and historical photographs.

As we explored the museum alone, surrounded by intriguing artifacts and exhibits, I took the opportunity to share my own story with Brandon. To my delight, he agreed to provide me with more in-depth information about Yaqui culture.

During our conversation, my curiosity deepened, and I couldn't help but inquire, "What does the term 'Pascua Yaqui' mean?"

"Pascua is Easter in Spanish. For our ceremonies during Lent, which occur from Ash Wednesday to Easter Sunday, Easter has always been a significant part of our culture, almost akin to the New Year for us. Easter Sunday represents the culmination of our year-long ceremony. The Lent ceremony spans 40 days. Easter, for us, symbolizes a new beginning—a fresh start in our approach to life, as we transition from one year to another."

"What is the history of your culture?"

"There isn't much recorded history before contact, referring to the time before Father Kino and the missionaries arrived. Our origin traces back to Mexico along Río Yaqui, a way to the south, and eventually, a fraction of the tribe migrated northward. Upon the arrival of the missionaries, our culture underwent a fusion with theirs. Hence, Yaqui culture represents a blend of Catholic beliefs and Indigenous Native American beliefs.

"What makes it unique is that we haven't completely assimilated, unlike some other Native American churches. We venerate saints in alignment with the Catholic orientation of religion, but we also hold onto other Indigenous beliefs rooted in Native values, emphasizing our connection with the Earth. Our tribe settled in the Tucson area in the late 1800s, early 1900s."

"Why do you think the Spanish colonization was such a success?"

"In the initial encounters with the Spaniards, things were more violent until the arrival of Jesuit missionaries. We became more open to dialogue as there were some similarities in our perceptions of a higher power. This facilitated communication and opened our community to a greater extent. The Jesuit missionaries respected our

116

Yaqui culture, and together we explored similarities to create something new.

"The collaboration was not forceful but built on mutual respect, in contrast to other cultures that faced punishment for their beliefs. The relationship followed certain rules, and missionaries introduced new foods and spices. Before contact, local foods were traded among the Yaqui, Pima, Mayo, and Tohono O'odham."

"What are the main specifics and symbols of your culture?" I probed.

"All tribes generally share the concept of reciprocity, emphasizing the importance of our connection with the land—a relationship we've always recognized as crucial. Our river held a sacred status, providing irrigation for our farms and crops, water for our people, and sustenance for our animals. Water, in our belief, is synonymous with life.

"Beyond the Catholic symbols, you can observe other symbols within our culture. For instance, the lizard is a symbol representing all animals. In our mythology, we acknowledge different worlds. 'Sewa' is the flower world beneath the dawn, home to 'Saila Maaso' or little brother deer. 'Huya Ania' is the wilderness world, and the lizard symbolizes this world, evoking a sense of respect, as originally, this is their domain. 'Tenku Ania' is a dream world, and 'Yo Ania' is a spirit world. We also have two darker mythological realms that shamans and curanderos can approach."

"Could you tell more about your ceremonies and the deer?" I asked hesitantly with humility, but deeply curious.

"In Yaqui, the term for deer is 'saila maso,' which translates to 'little brother.' When a deer appears, it emerges from the flower world, traversing through realms. In our ceremonies, it symbolizes the deer coming to bless our world. The dance unfolds throughout the night, and as dawn breaks, the deer returns to its world, having bestowed blessings upon our grounds.

"This dance is performed during land ceremonies, weddings, funerals, and facility openings. The dancer wears a deer's head to connect with the animal, along with rattles. The water drum mimics the deer's heartbeat, and rasps produce the sound of the deer's antlers. Historically, the deer dance preceded hunting expeditions, featuring a particular deer that could never be caught. Eventually, it revealed itself, adding a spiritual dimension to the tradition that has persisted for thousands of years."

Brandon, sensing my ever-growing interest, said, "Well, I have some time, so I can show you where we conduct the ceremonies. It's nearby." With that, we hopped into his car, and as we drove, he continued sharing deeper insights into the living traditions of the Yaqui people.

"What sort of dances do you have there?"

"So, there are many various ceremonies throughout the year for many purposes. Some of them are small ones, such as family gatherings with blessings, while the biggest one is the Lent."

I asked Brandon about Don Juan, a character in Carlos Castaneda's books who's portrayed as a key figure in Yaqui culture.

He responded, "We don't know about him in our community. Our shamans use various plants, but most of what Castaneda wrote is not part of our ceremonies.

"I think, it's based on a different tribe's cultures, and maybe Castaneda took mushrooms or peyote and had hallucinations that infused his writings."

"So, is it fiction?"

"No. I think it is a mix of truth and imagination. There is some truth to the medicines and to the region, but it is fictionalized. His stories are influenced by the use of hallucinogenic substances, which are not part of our tradition."

"I see."

His take on Castaneda seemed to me his clever way to contest it gently while not disparaging it at all.

We wandered around, exploring the community and ceremonial surroundings, and then walked back to the car. As we said our goodbyes, Brandon wished me luck on my journey and gifted me a tribal T-shirt with a deer dancer and a prominent sign stating "Old Pascua Village, est. 1922," honoring Yaqui land. I was moved by this personal connection and rich cultural insights he shared with me.

—

My subsequent days were delightful, starting with breakfast on the patio, followed by work, and then a hike in nearby Tucson Mountain Park. Alternatively, I would spend my time reading books on the terrace. Similar to Bob and Molly's house on the outskirts of town, this location invited occasional visits from wildlife, such as javelinas, and even one memorable encounter with a rattlesnake. The natural surroundings added an extra layer of charm to my stay.

As my understanding of the Yaqui culture deepened, I discovered the existence of the larger Yaqui reservation located south of Tucson, bordering Tohono O'odham tribal land. Further exploration led me to the knowledge that New Pascua Village has a cultural center known as Yoemem[4] Tekia Cultural Center And Museum. Fueled by my growing curiosity, I made the decision to explore the center in person.

For some reason, it was challenging to find, and my navigation led me to a different building. I decided to park in the middle and explore the newer community. After a short walk, I finally entered a small establishment that housed a restaurant, an art gallery, and a museum all in one. The space was decorated with colorful paper flowers, black and white photographs, and various pieces of Yaqui art.

A young woman named Rebecca greeted me at the entrance, and as we engaged in conversation, I shared details about my project. She suggested that I meet Raymond, one of the leaders who possesses extensive knowledge about Yaqui culture. Rebecca mentioned that he would be arriving soon for lunch. Intrigued, utilized the waiting time to explore the art show and peruse the historical photographs. In a matter of minutes, Raymond arrived.

Raymond proved to be very open and willing to share insights from his culture. After a brief discussion, we decided to plan a lunch meeting at the museum.

—

Raymond V. Buelna is a cultural leader of the Cristo Rey Church on the Pascua Yaqui Reservation in Tucson, Arizona. His role is to help preserve and advance the Yaqui way of life. Beyond his cultural responsibilities, Mr. Buelna serves as a community leader and has been a strong advocate for Indigenous rights at the Mexico-USA international border.

—

Raymond and I met at the museum a few days later. He graciously invited me for a delightful local-fare meal consisting of beans, rice, and spicier meat sauce. During our conversation, I shared details about my previous meeting with Brandon, and curiosity led

[4] Yoeme is the Indigenous term for Yaqui. Yoemem is plural.

me to ask about the differences between the Yaqui sub groups or villages.

"What distinguishes the Yaqui, Old Pascua Yaqui, and New Pascua Yaqui?"

"There is no difference in being Yaqui; we are all Yaquis. The only reason they call us Pascua Yaqui is that when we were seeking federal recognition, there were already Yaquis in Mexico, and the government needed to distinguish between Mexican Yaquis and U.S.-born Yaquis. Obviously, all of us are Yaquis throughout this region. We have always been in this area, and the border happened across us.

"Remember, all of this was Mexico, then the U.S. came and said we are taking it because they wanted to expand slavery. When it happened, Yaquis were fighting the U.S. government and the Mexican government too. Yaquis have always been fighting, and it has always been about this territory. Our main territory is in the Obregón area; that's where our life comes from, our home spot. However, that does not mean we wouldn't migrate or, more precisely, move within this area and between there and the Rio Yaqui Basin in Sonora, Mexico.

"Concerning the distinction between the New and Old Pascua, the original intention was that everyone would move to the reservation, but for some people, it was far away, and they wanted to stay in Tucson, mostly in the Old Pascua. That's why they are called Old Pascua, and the reservation is called New Pascua. There are around 600 people in the Tucson area and around 6,000 to 10,000 people here on the reservation. There are around 60,000 Yaquis living in Mexico around the Rio Yaqui Basin. The Rio Yaqui Basin stretches from Obregón, Sonora, all the way north to San Carlos, Sonora, west to the sea and east to the mountains. There are around 23,000 U.S.-born Yaquis who have officially enrolled with the U.S. Federally Recognized 'Pascua Yaqui Tribe.'"

"What is the purpose of the 40 Days Celebration of Easter, and what are the main characters of this ceremony?"

"Easter ceremonies are mainly about the pursuit and capture of Jesus. It's all Christian-based, honoring Jesus and his life during the 40 days leading up to his capture, persecution, death, and ascension. The ceremonies incorporate a symbolic reenactment that intricately weaves together Christian figures—Jesus Christ, Three Kings, and the four Marys—with pre-Christian Yaqui counterparts, including the deer dancer, Pascola or Pahkola, and musicians. These figures emerge to receive blessings, with the deer dancer assuming a spiritual role known to transcend realms. In Easter ceremonies, the deer dancer and Pascola dancer perform separately, yet their movements are harmoniously synchronized with the main ceremony.

"After Easter, on May 2nd and 3rd, Yaqui people celebrate the cross's ascension to heaven. May 2nd is dedicated to the Holy Cross, featuring specific prayers and a ritual where the cross is lifted through three staircases to symbolize ascension to heaven. Simultaneously, crosses are made from materials sourced from the river, particularly the bountiful weeping willow. In May, the weeping willow matures into large leaves, which are used to create crosses. These crosses stay in front of houses for a year, symbolizing a bountiful blessing from Mother Earth, bringing well-being and abundance."

"Who is the Pascola and why is his mask so important?"

"Pascola or Pahkola is the person who dances next to the deer dancer. He has a really important role. 'Pahko' is a word for ceremony, and 'O'ola' means old man. Together it means an old man of the ceremony, who has the responsibility to conduct it. He does prayers, gives narration, constantly yells, and provides words of encouragement to other participants, using a wooden mask. Masks are made from cottonwood root and represent various human characters and creatures such as goats, lions, and monkeys. They bring a respect for the animal world...

"The traditional symbols painted on a Pahkola mask represent ancient traditional knowledge that dates back ten thousand years. In the ancient past, the Yoemem were already engaged in farming and knew how to follow the movements of the stars and the moon for

122

planting and harvesting. They also utilized masks to transcend to a different place and time because they were responsible for prayer, meditation, and ensuring that the ceremony was aligned with its intentions.

"Pascola and all the musicians are tied together. Their songs are created to pay homage to the flower and animal worlds. The Pascola always starts off with the harp and violin, introduced by the Europeans, but we made our own version of the harp and violin.

"They play songs that mimic the sounds of Nature, like grasshoppers, butterflies, owls, and other beings. The deer dancer expresses all that and travels to other worlds. The water drum represents the heartbeat, the rattlers are the lungs, and the words that the singer sings bring it all together spiritually."

"What did your ancestors celebrate before Catholicism happened?" I asked curiously.

"Before Catholicism, we followed a seasonal calendar based on agriculture, gathering, harvest, and hunting during specific times. Everyday life throughout the whole year was woven around these ceremonies. In pre-Christianity times, we celebrated milestones in life, including war strategies, protection, and defense, as we also fought with other tribes. We were not always just living in harmony.

"But everything we did was connected to the respect of Nature and what Nature provided, and there was a specific timing to harvest items like cocoon rattles, deer horns, and deer heads.

"You can't harvest the deer head anytime. It has to be a specific time of the year. It changes color, the hair is different, their hair falls off, their hair stays on—there are all these different specifics and rules to understand and follow. It goes by timing.

"We use a lot of abalone shell. There is a time to get it, a time to harvest it, and a way to cut it. All of these things have to be respected and understood. It is a way to honor Nature and show respect; this was survival for us."

Raymond was very generous and kind to me. Thinking back about what he'd said about making war, I said, "The Yaqui in general seem to me a very kind people. You would have a right to be upset if provoked."

"You can't control what other people do, but you can control what you do. You know, and that is what it is to be Yaqui. But we can be mean too. It is a slippery slope. But mostly we don't want to be like that. All these values and how we react in difficult situations are a part of what we are all taught. That goes to your intentions for your day, and you carry it with you all the time.

"How you respond and who you are determines your day's outcome. In our greetings, we say 'Lios em Chania Vu,' with a handshake asking, 'How did the Creator treat you today?' Responding with 'Lios Em Chiokoe', means 'The Creator treated me well.' Another greeting is 'Kechim Allea' asking if you're happy, and we reply with 'Ke Tu'i,' meaning 'everything is good.' These greetings aim to foster closeness to the Creator and the person next to you. Our values revolve around Nature, people, respect, harmony, and love—the teachings of the Yaqui people. Love, respect, and community are our goals. Yaqui people pray daily with Alva de Dios, Santa Maria and Alva Maria prayers.

"All of these prayers start from morning to welcome the sun. Afternoon prayer—Santa Maria is to Mother Mary to think about your day, and what you are doing and nourish your body. The evening one is about reflection. The first one has a lot of intentions, well-being, having food, taking care of each other, and there are intentions for others. And they are intentions about what good you could do with your day and the gifts you personally might give.

"All those are intentions that you pray every day, and the second part is how are you doing on those intentions and how can you be better. The last one is Alva Maria to close out our intention for the day, and pray for the night, because bad things can happen during the night. Things which we can't see. This is in the evening prayer and that takes us to the next day. All of those things together are the

Yaqui way of life. You do it every day and this way you build this life with good intentions, with good thoughts, with good spirits, with well-being, and with your pure heart. And you contribute not only to your life, but also to your community."

With his generous sharing of these many spiritual practices, it gave me the courage to ask, "What is your origin story?"

"The Talking Tree is a Yaqui creation story featuring Yomumuli, a young lady, and her brother. While picking berries, they encountered a tree that exhibited unusual behavior and spoke a different language. Despite their amazement and fear, they understood the tree's message. It foretold the arrival of Spaniards, trains, automobiles, planes, and a different way of life for the Yaqui people. The tree emphasized the need for the tribe to decide whether to embrace a new life with new people or continue their traditional way of life in harmony with Nature.

"When Yomumuli and her brother shared the experience with their parents and elders, they were initially disbelieved. The tribe convened to discuss the revelation, eventually splitting into two groups. The Surim people, the original Yaqui, transformed into the Yoeme, the current Yaqui people. The other group of Surim transformed into various animals, such as ants, lizards, fish, and butterflies. These creatures are considered ancestors, once part of the Yaqui family.

"The Talking Tree story is not just a spiritual narrative; it is seen as a real account. The story underscores the importance of connection to Nature, akin to the connection the young girl had with the tree. It mirrors the interconnectedness of all things to Nature, reminiscent of the concept depicted in the movie 'Avatar,' where trees are portrayed as sentient beings with a deep understanding of the world around them."

I listened with fascination, absorbing the richness of Yaqui culture. As our conversation naturally came to a close, we had to have a moment of silence, appreciating the depth of what had been discussed. Raymond, generously offering a personal tour of the museum, provided additional insights into the cultural artifacts and exhibits.

The most significant gift was his next gesture—Raymond granted me permission to publish a copy of the Yaqui Origin Story. This act of trust and openness meant a great deal to me, marking the culmination of a meaningful exchange and a deeper connection to the Yaqui community. It was also a confirmation for me that spirit guides were truly helping.

THE TALKING TREE

(The Yoeme History - Oral Tradition)

Once upon a time, a long time ago, Itoma Achai Taa'a (our Father Sun), gave the Surem the land along the Rio Yaqui, in Sonora, Mexico. The Surem were little people, the wise ones, ancestors of the Yoemem, Yaqui people. The people were to take care of the land and their culture would live forever.

The Surem lived in what is now northern Sonora, and they were very quiet people. They lived close to nature and could communicate with animals. They were afraid of loud noise and would run and hide when there was thunder and lightning.

One day, the people heard a strange noise that seemed to come from a tree. The tree was ancient, and it was growing in the middle of the Surem region. It vibrated with strange sounds, as if it were speaking in another language.

When the villagers gathered around, the leaders tried to understand this "Talking Tree." It was no use. No one could understand what it was that it was saying. Not even the oldest leaders could understand.

Meanwhile, a young girl named Yomumuli Seahamut told her father that she could understand the "Talking Tree". At first, her father paid no attention to her because little girls were not supposed to know more than elders. Then the father became angry when the girl insisted.

"Alright, you do it in front of the village, but if you are only being foolish, then you will be punished," said her father. Yomumuli Seahamut sat down close to the tree and told them everything the tree said. The "Talking Tree" was predicting what would happen to all people in the future, not only the Surem.

The "Talking Tree" said that light-skinned and light-haired people would come to Surem country in the future. There would be much bloodshed and suffering of the people.

Many would have to leave and go to the cold country-north, where there would be other light-skinned people who would help them. After many years, said the tree, the suffering would come to an end.

The "Talking Tree" said that a large, black monster would come through their land. It would spit out fire and smoke and would make a loud wailing noise. It would have one eye that would shine for a long distance in the dark. But, this iron monster would only be able to travel along a certain metal path, and could never leave that path.

The "Talking Tree" told of a big bird that would fly over the land dropping its eggs on towns, destroying houses and killing people.

These, and many other things did the "Talking Tree" tell the people. Now was the time, said the tree, that the Surem would have to make a choice to either leave this world, or stay to face the future.

The Surem talked about predictions of the "Talking Tree". Then they divided into two parties. Those who could not stand such a future decided to go away. A Farewell Dance was held for them. Some people say that these Surem went into the sea and are still there. Others say that they took the form of ants and underground animals and still live underground in the hills.

Those Surem who stayed, grew taller and changed into the Yoemem that they are now. "Yoeme" means "the people", and is the name still used among the people. The Yoemem lived in seven villages—each village dedicated to one star in the Big Dipper. These villages in Sonora are along the coast of Guaymas. Each rancheria or cluster of houses held its own religious ceremonies of "Pahko".

At these pahkos, there were dances performed to thank Achai Taa's (Our Father Sun) for providing for these people. The sun, the people said, is the source of all our spiritual and physical energy, because our Creator lives there. There were deer and coyote dances, as well as many others, to show our respect for nature and life.

And as time goes on, the Yoemem still tell the predictions of the "Talking Tree".

(Blessings and grateful thanks to Raymond Buelna and the Yoemem Cultural Center and Museum.)

Refusal of Return

A profound sense of completion enveloped me, as if I had delved into one of the most ancient layers of existence.

Throughout this incredible journey, I underwent a transformation, becoming an agent much like a chameleon, seamlessly navigating through the diverse doors that the Sonoran Desert unfolded before me. Everyday life now appeared painfully dull, sharply contrasting the vivid adventures that had painted my existence. Through my personal experiences, everything in this extraordinary world felt alive and observant.

In my quest for understanding, I sought guidance from my shaman, Tereza. "What is expected from me now? Did I fulfill their expectations?"

"You did very well. It's time to go back."

"But I would like to stay…"

"You have to be where the Spirit wants you to be. Sometimes what we desire isn't what we truly need."

"Okay," I uttered, acknowledging the enigmatic forces at play.

"Maybe you are needed back home now," she suggested.

"I understand," I replied, slowly internalizing the notion that my mission had truly come to an end.

The sun, stars, mountains, birds, wildlife, cacti, horses, colors, warmth, Native Americans, cowboys, caves, tacos, festivals, music, and all my adventures—everything I now held dear—I had to part with as I braced myself for the return to the gray tones of Prague.

Selling my car and stepping onto the plane, an indescribable sensation lingered—a piece of my soul remained embedded in the vibrant landscapes of the Southwest.

My reluctance to return manifested as a bittersweet farewell to a chapter that had seamlessly woven itself into the fabric of my identity.

I felt akin to a naked, screaming root entrenched in the beautiful red clay, forcibly removed and transplanted elsewhere. The transition mirrored shedding a vibrant, desert-colored skin, only to be enveloped in the cold, gray-skinned reality awaiting me at Prague.

Master of the Two Worlds

I was overwhelmed by a deep feeling of grief. The second self that had remained here during my time away now felt like a stranger, and I yearned for Tucson with a substantial, almost painful, intensity. As I wandered vacuously along the banks of the Vltava River, I found occasional solace in the sight of the Charles Bridge.

In my search for understanding, I stumbled upon books about mysticism, legends, and captivating stories. Among these literary treasures, The Hero with a Thousand Faces by Joseph Campbell stood out. As I delved into Campbell's words, a realization dawned upon me—I had embarked on my own personal Hero's Journey. It was a transformative adventure into a supernatural world filled with trials, revelations, and incredible individuals.

The remarkable people I encountered in Tucson had a significant impact, and the private conversations I shared with each one of them were precious, profoundly altering me. These people had one thing in common—they dedicate ample time to the desert, establishing a profound connection with Nature. Their depth of character is derived from their bond with the natural world.

I firmly believe that nurturing such a relationship is the key to our collective progress, transcending individual differences and backgrounds.

At the end, the journey left me pondering: Did I play a role in healing the land, or was it the land that healed me?

One undeniable truth emerged—I absorbed the essence of Tucson and became a bridge, just as Tereza foresaw. I came to realize that I could navigate both worlds. This transformation surpassed any initial expectations or hopes I harbored when I first stepped into Tucson—and I hope I will return soon.

Acknowledgements

I extend my gratitude to Tereza Pohlova, who sent me on this life quest and mentored me. Special thanks to Molly and Robert Benham for their friendship and the luxurious accommodation they provided. Sincere appreciation goes to my mom for her steadfast support.

Deep thanks are extended to everyone I encountered on this transformative journey of self-discovery. Without the generous gift of their precious time and deep knowledge, my personal journey could not have come as far, and would have remained much less colorful. Most importantly, without the verbal sharing of gifts from these dear Tucsonans, this book could simply not exist!

Many thanks to Martha Ames Burgess for editing, providing a beautiful stay in her home; Andrea Rodriguez for a lovely painting on the cover; Daniel Clint for the illustrations; and Hanna Ripp for her networking skills.

My friends Forest Starr, Renae Lauterbach, and Nicole DeHaven deserve appreciation for their time spent proofreading and their support.

I would also like to sincerely apologize to some of my Czech friends with whom I lost communication. During that time, I found it challenging to articulate my experiences and the path I was on.

Recommended Resources

1) Desert Solitaire by Edward Abbey, ISBN: 978-0671695880

2) A Beautiful, Cruel Country by Eva Antonia Wilbur-Cruce, ISBN-10: 0816511942

3) The Sonoran Desert: A Literary Field Guide by Eric Magrane and Christopher Cokinos, ISBN: 978-0816532826

4) A Natural History of the Sonoran Desert by Steven Phillips and Arizona-Sonora Desert Museum, ISBN: 0520287479

5) A Natural History of the Santa Catalina Mountains, Arizona; with an Introduction to the Madrean Sky Islands by Richard C. Brusca and Wendy Moore, ISBN-10: 1886679487

6) Arizona: A Celebration of the Grand Canyon State by Jim Turner, ISBN: 1423607422

7) Gathering the Desert by Gary Paul Nabhan, ISBN: 9780816510146

8) A Desert Feast: Celebrating Tucson's Culinary Heritage (Southwest Center Series) by Carolyn Niethammer, ISBN-10: 0816538891

9) Tortillas, Tiswin, and T-Bones: A Food History of the Southwest by Gregory McNamee, ISBN: 0826359043

10) With Good Heart: Yaqui Beliefs and Ceremonies in Pascua Village by Muriel Thayer Painter, ISBN: 978-0-8165-4035-8

11) At the Border of Empires: The Tohono O'odham, Gender, and Assimilation, 1880-1934 by Andrae M. Marak and Laura Tuennerman, ISBN: ISBN-10: 0816521158

12) Tucson: The Life and Times of an American City by C. L. Sonnichsen, ISBN-10: 0806120428

13) The Desert Smells like Rain, a Naturalist in O'odham Country by Gary Paul Nabhan, ISBN: 9780816546893

14) Tucson, a Short History by Charles Polzer, ISBN: 9780915076116

15) Davis & Russell's Finding Birds in Southeast Arizona by Tucson Audubon Society Publications Committee, ISBN: 0964503107

16) Crossing the Line by Linda Valdez, ISBN: 9780875656182

17) High Tide in Tucson: Essays from Now or Never by Barbara Kingsolver, ISBN-10: 9780060927561

18) Rainwater Harvesting for Drylands and Beyond by Brad Lancaster, ISBN: ISBN-13: 978-09772464-5-8

19) The Desert Year (Sightline Books) by Joseph Wood Krutch, ISBN-10: 1587299011

20) Where Clouds are Formed by Ofelia Zepeda, ISBN-10: 0816527792

21) Selected Poems, 1969-1981 by Richard Shelton, ISBN-10: 0822953439

22) The Hero with a Thousand Faces by Joseph Campbell, ISBN-10: 1577315936

23) Resistance and Collaboration, O' odham responses to U.S. invasion by J.D. Hendricks, WWW: https://dn790009.ca.archive.org/0/items/VariousPdfs/Collaboration_and_Resistance.pdf

Tribal Donations

If you have an interest in supporting local tribes, consider exploring their cultural centers, browsing through their distinctive gift shops, acquiring their art, or making a donation to contribute to their communities.

Tohono O'odham

Tohono O'odham Nation Culture Center and Museum

Baboquivari, Mt Rd, Sells, AZ 85639

www.himdagki.org

Pascua Yaqui

Old Pascua Museum & Yaqui Culture Center

856 W Calle Santa Ana, Tucson, AZ 85705

www.facebook.com/TheOPMuseum

Yoemem Tekia Foundation

4721 W Calle Vicam, Tucson, AZ 85757

www.yoememtekiafoundation.org

"By this, the dreamer crosses to the other shore. And by a like miracle, so will each whose work is the difficult, dangerous task of self-discovery and self-development he portered across the ocean of life."

-Joseph Campbell